rhododendrons
camellias and
magnolias
2013

Royal
Horticultural
Society

Published in 2013 by
the Royal Horticultural Society,
80 Vincent Square, London SW1P 2PE

ISBN 978 1 907057 39 7

Designed for the RHS by Sharon Cluett

Edited for the RHS by Simon Maughan

Honorary Editor for the Rhododendron,
Camellia and Magnolia Group
Pam Hayward

Printed by Page Bros, Norfolk

COVER ILLLUSTRATIONS
FRONT COVER: *Rhododendron kesangiae*
AEB187 (Sally Hayward)
BACK COVER (*TOP*): *Camellia* x *williamsii*
'Exaltation' (Sally Hayward)
BACK COVER (*BOTTOM*): *Magnolia* 'Peachy'
(Sally Hayward)

Royal
Horticultural
Society

Contents

Chairman's Foreword

ANDY SIMONS

IN WHAT IS ALMOST CERTAINLY my last introduction to the Yearbook as Group Chairman I am keen not to dwell too much on the ongoing saga of the Group and the RHS. I would rather look to discuss wider Group and related issues. However, I regret it will not be possible to omit the governance discussions as they are so fundamental to the Group going forward, and, after all, this is the Group's Yearbook. Indeed, I was much taken and heartened by the interest shown by ordinary members when I spoke briefly on the subject of Group administration during the most recent Autumn Tour.

As I have indicated previously, I often try to consider the Group as a business. Not a business that seeks to make a dividend for its shareholders but rather one that looks to provide good service to its customers, in this case you, the members, at a minimum cost. Against this measure of success, I think we continue to perform well. Indeed, as I indicated in one of last year's Bulletins, each member is receiving more out in terms of publications etc than they are remitting through their subscriptions. Clearly this is not a situation which will be tenable going forward, and a more considered approach to Group finances, resourcing and subscriptions will be one of the challenges for our Committee in the next year or so.

Turning to the physical benefits of membership, the Yearbook and Bulletin continue to be a great success, and I would like you all to think hard about where these publications come from as you read them. They are not produced by some high end professional publishing house, nor do they appear by magic at the push of a computer button, they are actually a result of our two volunteer Editors committing a huge amount of their personal time for absolutely no recompense, other than satisfaction in supporting the Group. The other members

MAGNOLIA 'BANANA SPLIT'

SALLY HAYWARD

of the Committee also need a pat on the back, particularly those filling the roles of Treasurer, Membership Secretary, Tours Organiser, Seed Convenor and Webmaster, as they are even more unsung than our Editors. Group Tours have again been a great success this year. I attended the Autumn Tour and it was exceptional. Consider the treat of having grapes cut for us from the Chatsworth House greenhouses, worth the cost of the tour alone.

I know that I have said this before but unless you tell me and the Committee what you want from the Group it is impossible for us to do anything other than what we think is best. Input on large courses of action or the most minor of points is always welcome; nothing is trivial if it concerns you and a small change may have a big impact. With respect to the Committee, we have struggled to fill a couple of crucial roles that have fallen vacant this year, in particular that of Honorary Secretary. Please consider putting your name forward if you feel able to take on an active role – the only qualification necessary is enthusiasm, and the demands on your time would be as much or as little as you can afford to give.

Changing tack onto plant issues and in particular, plant health again, recently we have seen yet another national scare over trees dying out and now it is our ash trees that are threatened. It appears that a whole host of temperate and tropical tree species globally are under threat, with the mortality of mature trees far outpacing scope for regeneration. Clearly this growth in plant disease is being brought about by a number of factors, be they directly man-made or through a more subtle and less obvious set of reasons. The importation of infected plant materials is quite evidently a root cause of the rapid spread of some diseases. However, plants and seeds have been moving around the world routinely since at least the 18th century and with almost industrial vigour; tobacco, breadfruit and rubber are all examples. Bringing together the two thoughts of a reported rapid increase in plant disease and the fact that plants have been moved between countries for at least 200 years causes me to conclude that the simplistic reports of a certain disease being imported and causing a catastrophic outbreak are exactly that – simplistic. International communication is not going away and the expectation that alien disease is going to be kept at bay by regulation or border agency officials is wishful thinking at best and, at worst, we are deluding ourselves that a complex set of problems can be solved by a simple solution. Whilst we must all try and be really vigilant in keeping our eye out for these diseases and perhaps invest half an hour on the internet learning what to look for, what is really required is systematic scientific research into the problems. This research issue is the point that has really stirred me into writing this piece: I am really bored by so called 'research' on this subject that is little more than counting the number and type of dead trees and how they might or might not have become infected. Where are the major environmental studies into the causes behind the aggressive nature of these diseases and, most importantly, the work to develop prevention, treatments and cures? After all, we are not dealing with a narrowly impacting disease such as Camellia Petal Blight. These are problems that will change our environment at a really fundamental level. I recognise that such research is probably not of great interest to the private sector and that public funding needs to compete across all areas, but what value would you place on the diversity of our woody plants?

On a happier note, it is self-evident to me that the Group, both at main committee level and throughout its branches has been pro-active this last year in its primary objective of providing events and opportunities of interest and enjoyment, related to our three genera, for our members. Undoubtedly, the event of the year was the Spring Tour to Italy, for the success of which we have to thank Judy Hallett. The focus here was understandably on magnolias and camellias, although rhododendrons and many other exotic plants were enjoyed.

The highlight for rhododendrons was the superb display that helped fill the Rosemoor Marquee in April at the Main Rhododendron Competition and Show, supported once again by the excellent SW Branch Camellia and Magnolia Competitions. This was nicely balanced with the colourful display of late flowering rhododendrons at Jermyn's House in Hampshire in June, well organised by our New Forest Branch, Exbury Gardens and the Hilliers' team. There were successful shows, also in April, organised by our SE, NW and Wessex Branches, and the Bulletin gives evidence of the variety of garden visits available to our members during the year.

Turning to another benefit we provide – the Seed List – members now have the facility of downloading this as soon as it is available, and the 2012 list, all credit to our various collectors and suppliers, was a particularly rich one.

Returning to Group organisation and governance, as many of you will now know, we have gone through some significant changes in how the Group organises itself and relates to the RHS. It has been fortunate that the Group Committee has been able to isolate the membership from these changes and continued with the Group's principal business uninterrupted. This has not been an enjoyable or palatable experience for the Committee, as our interests are the same as yours – plants not administration. Regrettably, the process of reorganising the Group is destined to continue for another year as our relationship with the RHS evolves. Expect to see further work on the Group Constitution and a new formalised relationship with the RHS backed by a partnership agreement. The implications for the membership are again likely to be minimal but you may see a subtle name change and some alternative branding to go along with the new Constitution. As for the Group management, these changes will allow us to look hard at how the Committee is structured and it is likely that recommendations for a smaller Committee will be brought forward which will mitigate the need for some travel and hopefully reduce time wasted and costs.

Finally I would like to thank all of you who have supported me over the last three years and I hope to see you in the garden soon.

Editorial

PAM HAYWARD

AS I GET TOWARDS the closing stages of putting this publication together each year, a particular sensation begins to creep over me. Maybe it's the comfort of knowing that I am nearly in sight of the conclusion of what is a very demanding exercise or perhaps it is the sense of wholeness that comes from creating a book from an assemblage of many parts over many weeks that explains it; I'm not sure. What I am sure of is that each and every contribution to the yearbook assumes a very personal importance and each affects me in turn as I seek to present the ideas and information to you, the reader, in the most effective way. The process is, quite simply, a creative 'experience' akin to giving birth and with all the attendant emotions along the way!

This edition could indeed be an exposition of the word 'experience' and its various applications, from the transcendent to the practical, the positive or painful, and ultimately to the acquisition of wisdom to be passed on to the 'inexperienced'.

Consider Rama Lopez-Rivera's account of summiting Wa-Shan: here we have a young plant hunter recounting how he became the first foreigner to complete this particular journey since EH Wilson over a century before him. The evocation of his 'experience' of the overwhelming richness of the flora around him at the summit, conveyed in his own words and brought closer through his images, is a reminder of just how wondrous the natural world still is.

How very different is the 'voice of experience' with which Peter Cox speaks as he describes his return visit to China – not in the least bit jaded or dismissive but relaxed, business-like and coolly confident within his sphere of long-gathered knowledge. Refreshing, though, to hear that even such a seasoned traveller is not altogether immune from the captivating effect of the dramatic landscapes encountered on his trip.

Then again, there is Joseph Rock, a meticulous and prolific collector of astonishing quantities of material from the wild; his painful experiences as a child produced the man – solitary, driven and absorbed, totally self-disciplined; ideal qualities for his chosen profession. Just how much the rhododendron world, in particular, has benefited from his life is very evident in the images accompanying Charles Lyte's enlightening description of this complex individual and his work.

With our feet on more familiar ground, among the cultivated plants of the garden, 'experience' takes on a different meaning.

The five holders of National Collections of Magnolias have come together to describe their individual experiences of this responsibility. This has been a fascinating exercise: these gardeners, some of them unaccustomed to writing at length, have dug deep to produce a thought-provoking piece, revealing similarities and contrasts and some really quite unexpected aspects of this shared role. What is deeply satisfying is their common respect for the heritage and future of their collection and the wider garden that holds it. Of benefit to all magnolia growers, though, is the weight of experience brought to bear on reassuringly universal frustrations and the tried and tested remedies developed to deal with them.

Barry Starling's credentials hardly need presenting when it comes to experience – he is without peer in all things ericaceous and his wonderful venture into the world of bigenerics, made all the more enjoyable by recounting his son's early literary promise, simply emphasises how fortunate we are he has taken to the typewriter once more.

Neville Haydon is a veteran in the world of camellia hybridization, and his long service to the genus continues to enrich the legacy of hybrid gems for our delight. The depth of his experience is clearly seen in his ability to refine his hybridising palette to star quality parents and follow up with a razor sharp eye for the exceptional. He has produced outstanding camellias of all types but his work towards varieties suitable for smaller gardens and now to develop forms which are disease resistant is surely of the greatest importance. Some of his creations are already in our gardens and the fact that more are being trialled for UK suitability is excellent news for all camellia growers.

For a quarter of a century Caroline Bell has been growing and studying camellias, with a particular interest in scent – not just in terms of varieties but also in determining a satisfactory scientific explanation of its presence or otherwise. Her article is an exceptional piece of work which represents a perfect marriage of documentary and empirical research. She has certainly enhanced my appreciation of camellias and I cannot wait to follow up her observations with some of my own when the camellias bloom this season.

Dipping his cautious toe into the deep end of the Olympic-sized pool that is the RHS Main Rhododendron Competition, just a few years ago, Russell Beeson is now very definitely 'experienced'. His encouraging words and down-to-earth advice are highly appropriate in a year when three more of the RHS rhododendron and camellia events make their way out of London. Heed his words and take the plunge yourself – you won't regret it.

Learning 'by experience' is an expression which often suggests that something that really mattered has been lost but, by way of compensation, a long term benefit has arisen.

Just over ten years ago, a deadly and previously unknown plant infection was found in the UK, the effects and consequences of which impacted rapidly upon all three of our genera. The 2008 yearbook described the science of *Phytophthora ramorum* in some detail and went on to explore the ramifications for our precious garden plants.

Thankfully, a decade on, much more is understood and the lessons learned have been instrumental in bringing about positive outcomes. In contrast to Ian Wright's shattering initial report, his update in this edition presents a sign of hope that we are at least developing effective strategies to safeguard our plant heritage against this particular infection and others seemingly waiting in the wings to wreak havoc.

Another hard lesson was learned through the loss of important rhododendrons raised in New Zealand. Recognising the situation too late to save some varieties, the New Zealand Rhododendron Association has itself been developing proactive strategies to curate, assess and propagate those worthwhile plants that are still in existence.

Taking a cue from others, similar work is going on at Tremough, capitalising on the nearby micropropagation facilities of Duchy College to ensure the survival of the famous Gill hybrids.

And having acquired all the experience that a lifetime of collecting, raising and cultivating rhododendrons can impart and demonstrated your loyalty to and passion for the genus, perhaps you have earned the right to put your tongue firmly in your cheek and poke fun at it. Tony Schilling, fresh from his two-part *Rhododendron arboreum* 'main course', does exactly that and provides us with a marvellous 'dessert' – don't take it to heart!

Once again, it has been a privilege to work with so many eminent authors and contributors and I thank them all for their time and effort in bringing this edition to publication. I hope there is something of interest for everyone.

A NOTE ABOUT THE FRONT COVER IMAGE

Rhododendron kesangiae **AEB187** was collected by Anne and Edward Boscawen on a botanical expedition to Bhutan in 1987, led by Keith Rushforth.

It was collected at 3515m, on the Thrumseng-la, East Bhutan, and raised and exhibited by High Beeches Gardens Conservation Trust.

Keith considered it to be a distinct species (until then it had been known as a hybrid of *Rhododendron hodgsonii*), and spent time during the 1987 trip collecting material to confirm its status. In 1989 it was duly named *Rhododendron kesangiae* DG Long & Rushforth, in honour of Queen Ashi Kesang of Bhutan.

This collection has only recently started flowering and this particular selection, shown here at the 2012 South East Branch Show, has large leaves with a plastered silvery indumentum.

A century in seclusion – climbing the Wa-Shan

RAMA LOPEZ-RIVERA

RAMA LOPEZ-RIVERA SETS OFF TO CLIMB TO THE SUMMIT OF WA-SHAN, the fourth foreigner to ever do so and the first since EH Wilson's ascent in 1903

DURING THE SPRING OF 2011 I travelled to Sichuan Province in Western China to explore three sacred peaks: Emei Shan, Wawu Shan & Wa-Shan (now Dawa-Shan). These peaks are located in an almost triangular formation at the distant edges of a wild and sparsely populated area of country, formally known as the Loalin or Wilderness by the Chinese.

Although all three mountains are of significant interest in their history and richness of species, it is the Wa-Shan that is perhaps the least known. In the last 130 years only six foreigners have ever visited the area and only three actually summited Wa-Shan before I did myself in 2011. This is not due to Wa-Shan being any less rich or interesting than the other mountains, in fact Wa-Shan was the origin of some of the best plant introductions of the highest merit: *Magnolia sargentiana* var. *robusta*, *Rhododendron insigne* and *R. williamsianum* to name a few. Equally interesting is the peculiar shape of the mountain, being almost completely flat sided and topped, rising 3236 metres and surrounded by many steep mountains and deep valleys. By comparison, Wawu Shan is also flat topped and of similar height, but its outline is in many places uneven compared to that of Mount Wa with its almost perfect shape.

Emei Shan's form is completely different to that of both Wa & Wawu, almost resembling a 3000m sloping wave, faced by giant cliffs of over 2000m. Of the three however, it is more due to Wa-Shan's remote and inaccessible nature that it was so seldom visited in the past.

The first foreigner to ascend Wa-Shan was Edward Colborne Baber in June 1878 during his exploration of Western China for the British Consul (he was also the first to ascend Mount Emei). Although he did not collect plant material, he did record a physical description of Wa-Shan that subsequent explorers (myself included) could not better. *'The upper story of this most imposing mountain is a series of twelve or fourteen precipices, rising one above another, each not much less than 200 feet high, and receding very slightly on all four sides from the one next below it. Every individual precipice is regularly continued all round the four sides. Or it may be considered as a*

EDWARD COLBORNE BABER, the first foreigner to ascend both Wa-Shan and Emei Shan

flight of thirteen steps, each 180 feet high and 30 feet broad. Or, again, it may be described as thirteen layers of square, or slightly oblong, limestone slabs, each 180 feet thick and about a mile on each side, piled with careful regularity and exact levelling upon a base 8000 feet high. Or, perhaps, it may be compared to a cubic crystal, stuck amid a row of irregular gems. Or, perhaps, it is beyond compare.'

The next foreigner to ascend the mountain was Antwerp Edgar Pratt, again for the British Consul and eleven years after Baber in 1889. He was severely restricted in his movements due to hostilities towards foreigners by Chinese student uprisings that were prevalent at the time. On his initial journey towards Wa-Shan along the Min River, arriving at the town of Kia-Ting-Fu (Leshan), he was forced to take refuge along isolated river banks, from gangs of angry students throwing stones (some as big as apples) at his boat. The captain of the vessel was unable to make any significant headway while they waited for these groups to disperse. Pratt was further inconvenienced after getting word from officials that the town in which he intended to resupply was full of students attending local examinations, and entering the town would most likely lead to Pratt being killed. He was thus advised by an official that he should not proceed to Wa-Shan and instead head for Chengdu. Pratt refused this stating he had the relevant papers and would carry on whether the official liked it or not. Relenting, the official eventually decided to send two armed guards with Pratt. To disguise himself as a Chinese, Pratt had his head shaved, got into Chinese clothes and donned an artificial pigtail attached to the inside of his cap. Successfully passing unrecognised by the mobs, he was obliged to make his way as best he could overland to Wa-Shan, without using the quicker river route. Not only would going overland have taken him over horrendously difficult terrain, it would have taken him through the tribal areas of the Lolos (Yi Minority People), who had a savage reputation for killing and kidnapping both Chinese and foreigners alike! Finally arriving at the town of Wa-Shan, Pratt was able to stay for the summer in a mission house that had been founded some years before by the French missionary Père Joseph Martin.

THE GHOSTLY VIEW OF WA-SHAN FROM THE SUMMIT OF EMEI SHAN

RAMA LOPEZ-RIVERA

Père Martin happened to be visiting the mission from his headquarters in Huang-mu-chang 200 miles away and informed Pratt that he was the only European since Baber to come to Wa-Shan, Père Martin himself probably being the first to ever enter the area. EH Wilson states that Pratt may have been accompanied to the summit by native collectors sent by the Irishman Augustine Henry to collect herbarium specimens and goes on to say that if this is true then their collections would have been the first plant material to come from Wa-Shan.

The last foreigner to summit Wa-Shan was the hawk-eyed Ernest Henry Wilson during July 1903 while working for Veitch. Wilson had Wa-Shan pointed out to him for the first time while on the distant summit of Emei Shan some 20 miles away. From Emei he said it resembled *'a huge Noah's Ark, broadside on, perched high up among the clouds.'* He was obviously fascinated by the size and shape of Wa-Shan commenting *'When it was first pointed out to me, 20 miles or so distant, I could not believe it was the mountain. It looked like a huge vertical precipice, its massiveness belittling its height. There is something peculiar about the mountain which detracts its height.'* Later, during his actual ascent of Wa-Shan, after staying at the same mission as Baber and Pratt, he describes the many distinct bands of flora layering the mountain, commenting in particular on the richness of rhododendron species towards the summit. Wilson also states that there was once a prolific occurrence of silver fir (*Abies fabri*) on Wa-Shan, most of which had been cut down and left as rotting trunks by the time he arrived there. The only major stands left were restricted to the summit.

It should be noted that Chris Callaghan and S.K. Png from the Australian Bicentennial Arboretum went to Wa-Shan in October 2009, but they did not make it to the summit. Their account can be read in the *International Dendrology Society Yearbook 2009.*

My own journey to Wa-Shan, in May 2011, was greatly aided by a better road system than that of Baber, Pratt and Wilson's time. So within three hours of leaving Chengdu city, accompanied by my guide and driver, I arrived at the village of Wuchi, the last settlement before the ascent of Wa-Shan is made. As soon as I came in sight of Wa-Shan, it was almost impossible to keep my eyes from it. Its shape was so absolutely peculiar, resembling a giant ship stranded in a sea of green mountains. I would later see Wa-Shan from the summit of Emei Shan, where it indeed looked like a giant ark perched above the clouds, exactly as Wilson described it from his own vantage point on Mount Emei.

WHITE BEAR VALLEY, the traditional route to Wa-Shan

RAMA LOPEZ-RIVERA

take us up to the base of the mountain and the entrance to the Wa-Shan Nature Reserve, at around 1800m. From there, the ascent could be made to the summit, some five hours away on foot. As we followed a level track used by local farmers to access their fields below the entrance to the reserve, we passed through thick groves of *Metasequoia glyptostroboides* trees that had been planted for a forestry crop. Following this, the path started to climb steeply as we (or rather I) huffed and puffed our way up through the now heavily cultivated farmland. Here the chief crops seemed to be cabbage and potatoes. Some of these fields were so steep it defied belief anyone would want to grow anything on them, and it reminded me how difficult life must be for people in these remote areas. Eventually, as we began to wind our way up out of the fields, we entered an area of sloping alpine meadow. This area started to prove very rich in perennials,

Wuchi village is home to a small family run hostel which serves the needs of Chinese hikers, mainly from Chengdu City. Many of these follow the traditional route to Wa-Shan, along the White Bear Valley, a dangerous but beautiful canyon, beginning from the Jinkou River, (a tributary of the Dadu River) before stretching some 14 miles to the base of Wa-Shan.

During the first evening, although surprised at seeing a foreigner in their village, we were invited home by the owners of the hostel. After an excellent meal, they informed me that I was the first foreigner they had ever seen in their village and thus the patriarch of the family insisted on drinking copious amounts of an unpalatable thick sweet wine with me. He also told me that the climb of the mountain was by a clear trail, but the ascent was in many parts highly steep and dangerous, due to falling rocks. He said I would also have to tackle a number of wooden ladders near the summit that were very old and rotten, and a fall from which would be a drop to one of the lower ledges some 1000ft below. It would be important to be aware of our footing.

Early the next morning, my guide and I left our lodgings, carrying packs heavy with food and equipment for the climb. We followed a track that ran through the village, which would

PRIMULA PULVERULENTA   RAMA LOPEZ-RIVERA

quickly taking my breath away. Large swathes of *Primula pulverulenta*, with its deep pink candelabra flowers riding high above its light green leaves, grew near the stunning bluish-white flowers of *Iris japonica* with brilliant yellow and purple markings on each of the main petals. Also present were *Rodgersia pinnata*, *Cypripedium flavum*, *Astilbe grandis* and *Cardiocrinum giganteum*, its long stems approaching a metre high, but still a little early for flower. Interestingly these were growing in both the green-stemmed as well as the black-stemmed variety that I know from cultivation as *C. giganteum* var. *yunnanense*.

Pushing on, we began to enter the first belts of vegetation, in the form of thickets, rich in deciduous shrubs and small trees. These included the roses, *Rosa moyesii* and *R. chinensis* var. *spontanea* with long arching stems and deep-green glossy leaflets, making stunning specimens. I also found the white flowers of *Viburnum cordifolium* among the high spiny stems of the Chinese angelica tree, *Aralia chinensis*, as well as *Acer sterculiaceum* ssp. *franchetti*, *Sambucus javanica*, *Rhus chinensis* var. *roxburghii*, *Hydrangea anomala* and *H. aspera* ssp. *sargentiana* to name a few. Also prolific were wild strawberries, both in flower and fruit, along with *Urtica thunbergiana*, an Asian nettle known as 'Biting Cat' found throughout the region, and with a nasty sting similar to that of giant hogweed sap.

Next we passed through a dense belt of the beautiful bamboo *Fargesia nitida*. This important food plant for wild pandas is one of the most ornamental medium sized bamboo species found in gardens. On Wa-Shan it has attractive purple tinted arching canes up to about 8–9ft in height. From here, we moved into a wide belt of scrub that contained a number of deciduous woody species much the same as those mentioned earlier, but with the addition of

members of the *Fagaceae*, along with *Betula delavayi*, flush with yellowish-gold new leaves. Also present was *Rosa sericea* ssp. *omeiensis* f. *pteracantha*, with its stunning stems with deep-red flat sided thorns. I was constantly reminded of Wilson's account of his own visits to this mountain and was struck by how little had changed in the intervening century.

After a final push along a gradual section of track, we had an absolutely phenomenal view

THE DRAMATIC APPROACH TO WA-SHAN   RAMA LOPEZ-RIVERA

of Wa-Shan as we approached from the western end of the mountain. It seemed like the giant bow of a ship rising up ahead of us. As we approached, we could clearly see its almost flat-sided face with the countless, inaccessible tiers of rock so unique to Wa-Shan.

Rounding a final bend in the track, we arrived at the base of the mountain. Here a large sign in Chinese informed us that we had indeed entered the Wa-Shan Nature Reserve, also stating that the cutting of wood was strictly forbidden and that it is a dangerous mountain, and hikers who proceed do so entirely at their own risk (ie, don't bother calling for help).

We carried on via a single path towards the base through a sparsely wooded, marshy area that seemed to surround this side of the

TOP ROW, LEFT TO RIGHT: *IRIS JAPONICA* , *ACER CAMPBELLII* VAR. *FLABELLATUM*
MIDDLE ROW, LEFT TO RIGHT: *TRILLIUM TSCHONOSKII, RHODODENDRON* (possibly *R. AMESIAE*)
BOTTOM ROW: *BERGENIA OMEIENSIS*

RAMA LOPEZ-RIVERA

RHODODENDRON DENDROCHARIS growing epiphytically high up on a lichen-covered tree trunk

RAMA LOPEZ-RIVERA

mountain. Here we found a number of woody plants that had not been encountered so far, including *Magnolia sinensis*, *Rhododendron argyrophyllum* ssp. *omeiense* and *R. ebianense*, a handsome species in the Argyrophylla subsection, 8ft in height, with 10–12cm long, narrow elliptic glossy-green leaves. It had an attractive powdery white indumentum on the lower leaf surface and its open flowers were a pale pink.

The trail up Wa-Shan begins very steeply, with many turns through thick woodland, quickly needing both hands and feet to pull oneself upward. Flanked on each side was a mix of birch and oak along with a number of maples: *Acer campbellii* ssp. *flabellatum*, *A. caudatum* var. *multiserratum*, *A. sterculiaceum* ssp. *franchetti* and *A. pectinatum* ssp. *laxiflorum*. A few rhododendrons were starting to appear including *Rhododendron decorum*, *R. amesiae* and *R. calophytum*, the latter making particularly large plants 10–12ft in height and providing a little shelter for *Trillium tschonoskii* (and also for us from a light rain which had started!)

The going was tough as the steep trail made countless switchbacks, and after a good hour and a half we were now walking mostly in the open, along rocky paths. The weather had turned bad in a surprisingly short time, as we now hiked through heavy rain cloud and there was no chance of even a glimpse of what must have been spectacular views. Through breaks in the dense cloud I could see nothing but the sheer rock face of Wa-Shan, rising up out of the mist, first on one side and then the other. Here *Rhododendron dendrocharis* seemed to be completely at home, clinging to the most unimaginable positions in the rock and moss, along with a number of *Primula* species, while the path was now dominated by *Bergenia omeiensis*, which would follow us all the way to the summit.

After taking an unfortunate and slightly frustrating wrong turn along a path leading to

JUNIPERUS SQUAMATA   RAMA LOPEZ-RIVERA

small shrine, we had to retrace our steps to find the correct way. At this point my guide was obviously unhappy and suggested we set up camp for the night. At first I was reluctant, but considering the heavy rain and my guide's flimsy waterproofs, I relented in favour of a hot meal and the chance to dry off.

An uneasy night of being woken by the sound of falling rocks from above, left my guide's mood as unchanged as the weather. During breakfast I was completely taken aback when he told me he no longer wanted to carry on, and that I should continue to the summit on my own, suggesting that he stay and watch over the camp. In view of his lousy rainwear, I agreed and set off in the still heavy rain, under instructions to make it back to camp before nightfall. At 2800m, this meant I would have

RHODODENDRON PACHYTRICHUM
RAMA LOPEZ-RIVERA

to hightail it to get to the summit and back, leaving me little time to explore.

Within minutes of leaving camp I started to see the first conifers in the form of *Juniperus squamata* and *Tsuga yunnanensis*, the latter showing stunning white colouration on the undersides of the leaves.

Not long afterwards I arrived at the first of the wooden ladders that needed to be scaled to access the higher levels of the mountain. These were made from fir trunks leant side-by-side against the rock face with sticks tied onto them to act as steps. After scaling a number of these ladders between hiking, things started to get tricky as the path was becoming extremely narrow in places, with rock on one side and little else but air on the other. The last climb was by far the worst, requiring me to pull myself

TSUGA YUNNANENSIS   RAMA LOPEZ-RIVERA

over a steep rock with the aid of a single piece of galvanised wire, below which was nothing but mist and an unthinkable fall.

Within a few minutes of scaling the rock, it was obvious I had reached the flat top of Wa-Shan. The summit was dominated by the stunning fir, *Abies fabri*, now rising 30–40ft above me. Beneath these were countless rhododendrons, the sheer numbers were staggering. Working my way through them, I was quickly overwhelmed by the wealth of species, many of which were towering over my head. *Rhododendron pachytrichum*, *R. pingianum*, *R. oreodoxa* in stunning pink bloom growing near *R. maculiferum*, *R. longesquamatum*, *R. polylepis* and *R. dendrocharis* growing on the trunks of the fir trees. The small leaved

A WEALTH OF SPECIES ENRICH THE SUMMIT OF WA-SHAN *(ABOVE)*
AS WILSON RECALLED, THE *RHODODENDRON* FLORA IS PARTICULARLY IMPRESSIVE *(BELOW)*
RAMA LOPEZ-RIVERA

R. ambiguum grew alongside *R. argyrophyllum*, whose thick glossy green leaves showed golden brown indumentum on the undersides. Here also was *Rhododendron faberi*, *R. davidii*, *R. wiltonii*, *R. orbiculare*... the list just went on. My knowledge of this genus was quickly exhausted and it is to the great credit of David Chamberlain and Mark Flanagan that I have been able to identify rhododendrons through images taken at the summit.

A short while later I entered a truly enormous clearing of low grassland opening out into the mist (indeed like a giant park, as Wilson said). Even here rhododendrons were present with *R. nitidulum* forming hummocks, dotted through the grass.

RHODODENDRON OREODOXA

RAMA LOPEZ-RIVERA

RHODODENDRON LONGESQUAMATUM

RAMA LOPEZ-RIVERA

I took shelter from the rain in an old temple filled with various Buddhist ornaments, including a giant iron bell, as well as incense offerings and a multitude of small Buddhist figures. Also present were three, metre-high statues carved from fir trunks and colourfully painted in the form of a Buddha flanked on each side by bodhisattvas. Curiously, these were in a Mandarin style of dress and according to Professor Tim Barrett, an expert on Chinese history at the School of Oriental & African Studies, this is a unique style that he has never encountered before.

As I stood in the doorway of the temple looking out into the rain, I was able to enjoy the moment, reflecting on how little had changed on Wa-Shan since Wilson was here and the fact that I was the first foreigner to

stand at the summit of this magnificent mountain since Wilson himself and maybe the first to do so alone.

As I headed back down to the night's camp, I was left with a feeling of awe at this most special place and was already looking forward to my next encounter with the mighty Wa-Shan.

ACKNOWLEDGEMENTS

I wish to thank the following for their generous help and advice, without which this trip would never have been possible. Any inaccuracies are entirely my own. A special thanks to Mark Flanagan, Keeper of Gardens at Windsor, for providing references and history

RHODODENDRON DAVIDII

RAMA LOPEZ-RIVERA

OPEN PARKLAND ON THE SUMMIT with *Rhododendron nitidulum* in the foreground

RAMA LOPEZ-RIVERA

for my trip to Wa-Shan and for encouraging me to go that little bit further in my trips to East Asia; David Chamberlain of the Royal Botanic Garden Edinburgh for his assistance in rhododendron identifications; Tony Kirkham of the Royal Botanic Gardens Kew for his help and encouragement; William McNamara, Executive Director of Quarryhill Botanical Gardens for his assistance; Lisa Pearson, Keeper of the Wilson Archive at the Arnold Arboretum of Harvard University for access to Wilson's journals; Julie Carrington of the Royal Geographical Society for access to papers; Professor Tim Barrett of the School Of Oriental &African Studies; and Kid Wu of Hengxin Travel Service, Chengdu.

My sincere gratitude must go to Pam Hayward and the Rhododendron, Camellia & Magnolia Group, without whose generous support this trip would never have been possible.

REFERENCES ■ Fang, W-P. *Sichuan Rhododendron of China*, Science Press, Beijing, (1986). Pratt, AE. *To the snows of Tibet through China*, Longman's, Green and Co, (1892). Baber, EC. Travels and researches in western China, *Royal Geographical Society Papers*. Vol. 1 (1): 38., (1882). Wilson, EH. *Expedition Journal for Wa-Shan* (Arnold Arboretum). Bean, WJ. *Trees and Shrubs Hardy in the British Isles:* 8th Edition N–R Vol. 3, John Murray, (1987). Flanagan, M and Kirkham, T. *Wilson's China: A Century On*, Kew Press, (2010). Cox, EHM. *Plant Hunting in China: A History of Botanical Exploration in China and the Tibetan Marches*, Oxford University Press, (1945).

Rama Lopez-Rivera

is a plantsman and regular traveller to Temperate Asia to see woody plants in the wild

Fifty years of camellia hybridisation

NEVILLE HAYDON

MY CAMELLIA HYBRIDISING BEGAN in the early 1960s, when I read a series of articles by Tom Savige on various species. One of his many suggestions was to cross *Camellia rosiflora* with *C. tsaii*. Realising that both were in flower in my garden, I went straight out and made my first hand pollinations. These resulted in a seedling worth naming for its dwarf, rounded growth – *C.* 'Baby Bear'. Such surprising instant success led me on, and also gave me a particular affection for hybrids from the small leafed, mass flowering species. It also played some part in my later decision to leave accountancy and establish Camellia Haven as a specialist nursery.

The next registration was an anemone form *C. japonica*, which I named 'Takanini', to draw attention to the suburb of Auckland where the nursery was located. Its point of difference is a very long flowering season, starting in autumn. I could also pitch to customers that they were getting two plants for the price of one, most of the flowers being plum red, but at certain times

CAMELLIA 'BABY BEAR'

BEATE ZIMMERMANN

THE ORIGINAL PLANT OF *CAMELLIA* 'BABY BEAR'

NEVILLE HAYDON

changing to purple. The best of my other larger flowered introductions would be *C.* 'Nonie Haydon', a pink peony form *C.* x *williamsii*, and 'Peggy Burton', a seedling of the *pitardii* x *japonica* hybrid 'Nicky Crisp' with the same colouring, but larger and with more regularly placed petals.

All plant hybridising should have definite goals, and I decided to aim for early flowering plants other than *C. sasanqua* varieties, to extend the flowering season, and for small, compact plants suitable for the ever smaller areas allotted to city home gardens. *C.* 'Tarantella' is a promising *C. reticulata* type flower, which starts flowering in late autumn due to an infusion of one quarter *C. sasanqua*.

A dwarf form of *C. saluenensis* which I collected in Yunnan twenty years ago is

CAMELLIA 'TAKANINI'   NEVILLE HAYDON

CAMELLIA 'PEGGY BURTON'   NEVILLE HAYDON

retaining the very compact growth in most of its hybrids. I thought it worth naming for itself as *C. saluenensis* 'Haydon's Compact'.

My high regard for the small leafed hybrids also led me to promote them at the nursery, whether of my own breeding, such as 'Transpink', 'Festival of Lights', 'Seaspray' and 'Silver Column', or those produced by others, in New Zealand or from overseas. That has diversified the range of camellias on offer, and nurseries which produce standard camellias quickly found them very suitable for that form of plant. But I had no idea then that the small leafed hybrids would also lay the groundwork for rebuilding after disaster struck. No, not the Christchurch earthquakes which have so damaged that

beautiful city, but the arrival of fungal disease *Ciborinia camelliae*, or camellia flower blight.

A well-worn saying here is that almost every new plant that reaches New Zealand feels that it has reached paradise. The downside is that most newly introduced pests and diseases also reach the same conclusion and flourish accordingly. The arrival of flower blight has had a terrible effect on our camellia growing but the fight-back began immediately.

The Camellia Memorial Trust was established on the suggestion of Colonel Tom Durrant, also responsible for the formation of the NZ Camellia Society. The Trust operates as the research arm of the Society. Tom gave his autobiographical

CAMELLIA 'TARANTELLA'   NEVILLE HAYDON

A SELECTION OF NEVILLE HAYDON'S MINIATURE CAMELLIAS
TOP & MIDDLE RIGHT: **THE NEAT, FASTIGIATE HABIT OF** *CAMELLIA* **'SILVER COLUMN'** *(SASANQUA* x *FRATERNA* **'YOIMACHI') & ITS FREELY PRODUCED MINIATURE FLOWERS**
MAIN PICTURE: C. SALUENENSIS **'HAYDON'S COMPACT'**, a superb dwarf form with small leaves and miniature flowers – signature characteristics inherited by its hybrids *(BELOW)*
BOTTOM (LEFT TO RIGHT): **C. 'DESMOND HAYDON', C. 'KARAKA GEM', C. 'KARAKA CHARM'**

NEVILLE HAYDON

memoir the title 'Time and Chance', a biblical quotation very apt for someone from a UK estate agent family who became the youngest British Army colonel appointed in WW2, in charge of the vital Sierra Leone garrison, then involved in the Normandy invasion, and post-war emigrating to New Zealand, where he was prominent in farming, education and horticultural organisations. The RHS awarded him the Veitch Memorial Medal for his services to horticulture.

Since blight arrived, the Trust has devoted all of its attention to combating it. The Trust operates in the only way possible under its financial constraints, by funding students through Masters or PhD degrees at our agricultural universities, Massey and Lincoln. First came a 'know your enemy' project in which Christine Taylor studied the make-up of the disease, its life cycle and its variable effect on available species. An important result of her work was to establish that many of the small leafed species have defence mechanisms giving them partial or almost total resistance when spores land on their petals. Our present student, Matthew Denton-Giles, is continuing these studies by electron microscope, and also using DNA sequencing machines to try and discover which genes 'switch on' when they detect threat from spores. His is the largest project initiated by the Trust, with generous help from the Leslie and Gladys Riggall Foundation.

Our conclusion to date is that the way forward is to work further with the hybrids which, by observation, have clearly inherited resistance from the species parent, incorporating larger flowered cultivars and relying on the Mendelian inheritance laws to give us a percentage of resistant plants.

A Californian nurseryman, Daniel Charvet, has been doing that for twenty years, producing hybrids of very complicated parentage. Again, he did not do so originally to combat blight, but to develop very free-flowering plants, dropping their flowers early, and with good plant structure. Since being acquainted with the extra possibilities of his work, he has realised that many of his hybrids are in fact blight resistant. It was a blow to discover that importation of plant material from California would now be near impossible, but happily we are able to import

CAMELLIA 'TRANSPINK', a most attractive scented *C. transnokoensis* seedling with 3cm flowers, small leaves and a dense columnar habit

NEVILLE HAYDON

seed, and Daniel has very generously provided us with some hand pollinated seed with parents which have displayed blight resistance. His hybrids have up to three resistant species in their parentages, and we foresee them saving us from fifteen to twenty years work to replicate his efforts. To revive another old saying, if we had not found Daniel Charvet, we would have had to invent him.

Note: Trehane Nursery is currently trialling Neville Haydon's small leaved camellia hybrids.

Neville Haydon

is a renowned camellia breeder and nurseryman who gardens in Auckland, New Zealand. He is currently the International Registrar for camellias

Kalmioddities

BARRY STARLING

X *PHYLLIOPSIS* 'SWANHILDE' makes a fine display in the garden of the author   BARRY STARLING

IT WAS IN THE EARLY 1960s that I first read about *Kalmiopsis leachiana*, a choice small shrub from Oregon, USA. It had been discovered as recently as 1930 by Dr and Mrs Leach while horse riding in the remote wilderness of Curry County and proved to be a member of the family *Ericaceae* closely related to *Phyllodoce* and the European genus *Rhodothamnus*. As soon as I read about it I was keen to add it to my collection of dwarf ericaceous shrubs but efforts to track it down proved fruitless until, while on a visit to a Sussex nursery, I discovered that they had succeeded in propagating just three cuttings from their single plant. The nurseryman was not about to part with one of his precious rooted cuttings to a total unknown who would probably kill it and quoted twenty-five shillings for it

(remember that 25 shillings then would have purchased a seven year old chunky plant of a hardy hybrid rhododendron). Not put off, I made the purchase and never regretted it. The little shrub slowly grew to about 40cm diameter, 15cm high while its dense mass of 1.5cm long ovate leaves were completely obscured in April and on into May by over one thousand pink blossoms with a passing resemblance to *Kalmia*. Subsequently, I was able to obtain a little wild collected seed and managed to germinate and rear just one seedling.

In 1974, my wife, two young sons and myself launched an expedition to 'kalmiopsis country'. My eight year-old son described the expedition thus in a school essay, shortly after our return. Reader, allowance should be made for a vivid imagination and some degree of poetic licence. He had just scrambled ashore after losing both craft and provisions whilst shooting the rapids:

'I did not have anything except my clothes and pocket knife. I found some driftwood and carved it into shape and tied the logs together with some reeds. Looking round I saw a Lepped. It ponced on me and I dived for my pocket knife and stabbed it then used the skin on my raft. I slept on my raft and in the morning got up and ate the lepard meat. I lornched the raft and was always looking for a pink Kalmyopces. I saw a pink plant on the side and paddled over but it was not a Calmyopces. I tied up my raft. Next morning I woke up and went for a walk and saw a little pink flower behind a tree. It was the pink Calmeopcis so I dug it up and put it in a Polithing bag.'

Imagine the dilemma of the teacher, who I am quite sure had never heard of *Kalmiopsis*. Which of the three spellings was correct? Wisely, she played safe and let all three stand, for, after all, her concern was English, not Latin! I could not help wondering what permutation

KALMIOPSIS LEACHIANA in the *Kalmiopsis* Wilderness of southwest Oregon   MICHAEL KAUFMANN

of letters he would have used for the actual location of his 'pink flower' had he known it. For even if he had spelt 'Umpqua Valley' correctly would his teacher have believed him!

In reality we were only slightly intrepid. Our guide was Boyd Kline, an Oregon nurseryman, who was one of the original discoverers of the Umpqua population of *Kalmiopsis fragrans*. To get to the plants we had to wade across the Umpqua River, at this time of year all of 15cms deep in places, and then scramble up cliffs of porous, volcanic rock to a point where natural caves once housed American Indians. Here *K. fragrans* spread and sprawled over rocks in centuries old clumps. Tall pines gave dappled shade and the rock provided perfect drainage. It is interesting to note that *Kalmiopsis* is one of the few drought-resistant ericaceous shrubs. It is, however, susceptible to fungal infection at the root and this is often the reason for plants failing. Evolving in the sulphur-rich environment of this volcanic region, plants have never been exposed to diseases like *Phytophthora* and so have no resistance.

KALMIOPSIS FRAGRANS clings to the rocky slopes of the North Umpqua river along with *Arbutus menziesii*
DAVID McCLURG

Two named clones have been introduced from the Umpqua River colony. One called *K. fragrans* 'Umpqua River' was named by Harold Esselmont, of Aberdeen, when it obtained an

KALMIOPSIS FRAGRANS   DAVID McCLURG

Award of Merit from the RHS. Within a few months of receiving the award the plant died without ever having been propagated, so the plants presently labelled 'Umpqua River', although no doubt from that colony, are not, strictly speaking, entitled to that cultivar name. The second clone, *K. fragrans* 'Marcel Lepiniec', was named after a French emigrant who made Oregon his home and fell in love with its wild flora. It is said that he relied solely on liquor to sustain him during his forays and it was his friend, the aforementioned Boyd Kline, whom he trusted to get both him and propagating material of the kalmiopsis safely home again at the end of the day.

In fact the Umpqua plants are very diverse, ranging from tiny thyme-sized leaved plants to those of larger stature, with leaves up to 3cm long, 1.5cm broad. Flowers vary in size and have a colour range from palest pink to magenta red.

The type plant of *Kalmiopsis leachiana*, often referred to as Curry County form, discovered by the Leaches, comes from an area known now as the *Kalmiopsis* Wilderness which has as its only other claim to fame a high population of rattlesnakes – perhaps this is why our plant remained undiscovered for so long! Until a few years ago it was thought that the species was monotypic but in 2007 Robert J Meinke and Thomas N Kaye of Oregon State University published a paper giving separate specific status to the colonies of *Kalmiopsis* found in the Southern Cascade Mountains of Douglas County which includes those from the Umpqua River region.

The name chosen was *Kalmiopsis fragrans*, which puzzled those familiar with the plant as grown in Britain. Checking articles and plant encyclopaedia entries going right back to the discovery of the plant in the 1930s, none mentioned any fragrance of either flowers or foliage. In my 50 years of growing this species, at no time have I caught so much as a whiff of scent nor met anyone that has commented on this characteristic. Maybe the explanation is that the much warmer spring weather of south Oregon triggers the release of scent, a characteristic denied to those of us from more northern climes.

As a consequence of this change in nomenclature, when referring to the Umpqua kalmiopsis in this article, the name *Kalmiopsis fragrans* has been used.

KALMIOPSIS LEACHIANA 'GLENDOICK'
MIKE IRELAND

PHYLLODOCE BREWERI in the Donner Pass,
Sierra Nevada, California   BARRY STARLING

As successive generations have been reared in cultivation, propagation appears to have become easier. Where more than one plant is growing, seed is freely produced and germinates well. I sow in 10cm pots of half grit, half peat topped off with 1cm of sieved peat. The seed is sown on the surface and the pot stood in soak for a couple of hours after which it rarely needs further watering until after germination. Placed in a heated propagator, germination takes about one month and when seedlings are large enough to handle they are pricked out into trays and subsequently individually into small pots. If steady growth is maintained they can go out into open frames in June or July and a small percentage of seedlings will flower 15 months from sowing. Cuttings of shoots just beginning to firm up can be rooted in a two-thirds grit, one-third peat mix during summer and without additional heat. Most of the plants described below can be propagated in similar manner from cuttings.

Kalmiopsis leachiana has a reputation for being difficult to grow but one in my garden has survived on a dry bank for many years. Like the Umpqua plant, it is diverse in habit, inflorescence and flower colour but is generally taller, more open in habit – a metre high plant has been recorded – and bears flowers in elongated racemes of up to 20cm in length.

Peter Cox, of Glendoick, has crossed the two species of *Kalmiopsis* to produce a hybrid, *K.* 'Glendoick' which is robust, with a clear pink flower – this has proved a good garden plant.

While on a visit to Hillier's nursery in July 1971, I spotted a group of small shrubs labelled *Kalmiopsis leachiana*. By now I was pretty familiar with that little treasure and could see that these were totally different to anything I had seen before. After purchasing two of the mystery plants, which were both fairly straggly, I cut one back hard and repotted it. The second was planted out among dwarf rhododendrons and other small Ericaceae. By 1976 the pot-grown plant had made a handsome shrublet and by April of that year was flowering abundantly. Exhibited to the Joint Rock Garden Committee of the RHS it received an AM, subject to naming. Material was sent to Dr James Cullen at RBG Edinburgh who confirmed suspicions that this was a bigeneric hybrid between the type *Kalmiopsis leachiana* and *Phyllodoce breweri*. Roy Lancaster, Harold Hillier's right hand man at the time, proposed the name x *Phylliopsis hillieri* 'Pinocchio'. Why 'Pinocchio'? Like the animated doll of

X *PHYLLIOPSIS* 'PINOCCHIO'   BARRY STARLING

the children's story, our plant came from myster-ious, even magical origins. Subsequently I learned in conversation with Dr Brian Mulligan, director of Washington Arboretum, that he had sent Harold Hillier seed of the Curry County *Kalmiopsis*, from a plant in the arboretum growing adjacent to *Phyllodoce breweri*. In the wild these two plants are separated by a couple of hundred miles so it seems likely that the mating took place in the arboretum.

The second plant flourished in the open ground producing two crops of flower a year. Being a 'mule' it is sterile so devotes no energy to seed production – once over the first flowering it sets about producing a second crop. Oblong to ovate leaves are intermediate in size and shape between the two parents, having slightly revolute margins. The unique golden, glistening glands found on the underside of kalmiopsis leaves are present to a lesser extent in x *Phylliopsis*. Cup-shaped, mid-pink flowers with slightly reflexed corolla lobes are borne in elongated racemes predominantly in April/May but often again later in summer.

X *PHYLLIOPSIS* 'COPPELIA'   BARRY STARLING

Mike and Polly Stone, who created a beautiful *Ericaceae*-friendly garden on the shores of Loch Ness, made the same cross, raising a number of seedlings, one of which they named 'Askival'. Interestingly, this plant is almost identical to 'Pinocchio' but with me flowers a week or two later.

Inspired by 'Pinocchio', I crossed another species of *Phyllodoce*, *P. empetriformis* with *Kalmiopsis fragrans* from Umpqua Valley using the phyllodoce as seed parent. Among the seedlings were four very similar of exceptional vigour, very floriferous and differing from 'Pinocchio' in their more phyllodoce-like leaves and shorter, multi-flowered raceme. Compact inflorescences of 7 or 8cm diameter were composed of 1cm wide campanulate corollas, pink with just a hint of lavender, borne on slender, 1 to 2cm long pedicels. Remaining in the realms of fantasy and following Roy Lancaster's theme, the selected clone became 'Coppelia' after the life-size doll of the Sibelius ballet. This figure, of course, was created in the story by the eccentric Dr Coppelius and it has been unkindly suggested that my bigeneric hybrid was also the work of a crank!

x *Phylliopsis* 'Coppelia' received an AM in 1982 and in due course an AGM, encouragement enough for me to continue dabbling in bigenerics. Next in line to receive kalmiopsis pollen was *Phyllodoce glanduliflora*, a milky-white flowered species with a narrowly-urceolate corolla. This is a very hardy species from NW North America with the top of its range in Alaska. Just two seedlings resulted from this union and it was five years before the first of these flowered. It was a compact plant with tiny oval leaves and heads of small, pink-budded corollas which opened to white. The second seedling, which flowered the following year, is larger in all its parts and bears heads of

X *PHYLLIOPSIS* 'SPRITE'   BARRY STARLING

slender pink corollas 1.5cm long with five long, pointed lobes. Seeking names for these, it was suggested that 'Puck' and 'Sprite' might have the appropriate fantasy connection so the little white one became 'Puck' and the sparky pink one is 'Sprite'. After a few years I decided that 'Puck' was not up to scratch so did not distribute it, though the little spirit still lurks in a corner of my garden. Also I had misgivings about 'Sprite' especially when my next hybrid came on the scene, but it was too late, 'Sprite' had already escaped into the gardening world and has proved rather popular.

Next on the scene was x *Phylliopsis* 'Mermaid', looking like an enlarged version of 'Sprite'. This is *Kalmiopsis fragrans* crossed with the larger flowered, very hardy *Phyllodoce aleutica*, a creamy-yellow belled shrublet with a range from British Columbia to Alaska and down through the chain of islands to Japan. 'Mermaid', with buxom, flesh-pink corollas has lobes which taper in fish-tail form. In May a profusion of these flowers are just a little larger than those of 'Sprite' but blooms produced spasmodically during the rest of summer are often up to 2cm long, 1cm in diameter. 'Mermaid' is a vigorous grower and is one of the easiest to propagate.

A cross between *Kalmiopsis fragrans* and the circumpolar *Phyllodoce caerulea* produced x *Phylliopsis* 'Sugar Plum'. Large flowered, plum-shaped blooms sit atop a compact, rich green foliaged shrub which seems particularly susceptible to *Phytophthora* when grown in a pot, though open ground plants given good drainage will thrive for many years. At one stage it was touch and go whether 'Sugar Plum' would survive when the only stock plant collapsed and just a few unrooted cuttings remained in the propagator to secure its future. Although this hybrid is not well known in Britain it has enjoyed considerable success in Canada and the United States where it has been propagated by the thousand. Ironically, a wholesale grower not far from my abode proudly showed me a hundred young plants of 'Sugar Plum' informing me that this was a 'new American variety' that he had imported and obviously did not believe me when I claimed it as my baby.

TOP: ***PHYLLODOCE GLANDULIFLORA* 'FLORA SLACK'**
(SHOWN TWICE ACTUAL SIZE)
MIDDLE: ***PHYLLODOCE ALEUTICA***
BOTTOM: ***PHYLLODOCE CAERULEA*** in Norway
BARRY STARLING

X *PHYLLIOPSIS* 'MERMAID' BARRY STARLING

Although bigeneric hybrids are generally sterile, each year I would look for swollen seed capsules and occasionally would find them on x *Phylliopsis* 'Pinocchio'. When seed from these germinated, often distorted, non-flowering plants would result but in one instance a strong, vigorous seedling appeared. It resembled a kalmiopsis though larger in all its parts – a super kalmiopsis, in fact! Its flowers, plentifully produced, are rich pink and continue over a long period. This I named x *Phylliopsis* 'Hobgoblin' after the occupants of nearby Hobhouse quarry who regularly steal and hide my tools while I am working in my garden. 'Hobgoblin' proved fertile and seedlings from it inherited its size and vigour, flowering in a range of colours from palest pink to rosy-red.

X *PHYLLIOPSIS* 'HOBGOBLIN' SEEDLING

BARRY STARLING

At the time of making the 'Coppelia' cross both the kalmiopsis and phyllodoce parents were selected randomly but more recently I decided to repeat the cross using a large-flowered, pure pink kalmiopsis and *Phyllodoce empetriformis* 'Martin's Park', the best form of that species growing here. It was collected in the Olympic Mountains by Dr and Mrs Brian Mulligan and bears large inflorescences of clear pink bells. From this union two seedlings looked worth perpetuating. Their performance equals that of 'Coppelia' but, with more and larger flowers to the truss and a pink with no blue in it, they have the edge. One, named x *Phylliopsis* 'Titania' has flowers of a clear mid-pink while the other, x *Phylliopsis* 'Swanhilde', is a lighter pink with up to 25 flowers making

X *PHYLLIOPSIS* 'SUGAR PLUM' BARRY STARLING

up each inflorescence. Those familiar with the ballet *Coppelia* will remember that it is the real-life beauty, Swanhilde, that the hero marries and lives with happily ever after, realising what a twerp he had been in falling for a robot doll.

About twenty years ago seed arrived from a *Phyllodoce empetriformis* found growing on Steven's Pass in the Cascade Mountains of Eastern Washington. Plants from this seed flowered purple red and it was not long before its potential as a x *Phylliopsis* parent struck me. Here was a new colour that would add a richness to the tapestry of hues woven by a planting of these little ericaceous oddities. Easier said than done! Almost every year for the next ten years I attempted a cross using

X *PHYLLIOPSIS* 'PURPLE EMPEROR'

BARRY STARLING

Kalmiopsis leachiana 'Hiawatha' – the reddest of the kalmiopsis – as pollen parent. Sometimes no seed would be set while on other occasions good-looking seed would not germinate or seedlings would fail within a couple of months of germination. Two seedlings survived for six months and one year respectively and then succumbed. Finally a seedling grew on and after five years flowered, living up to expectations. Short racemes of 1cm diameter purple-red flowers, each borne on a slender deep red pedicel up to 3cm in length, had not only cup-shaped corollas of this rich hue, but the styles, anthers and calyces were of the same colour. A name was not hard to find – x *Phylliopsis* 'Purple Emperor' seemed to fit the bill and survival of the hybrid is now secured by the rooting of a good batch of cuttings, some of which are now in the hands of other growers.

When *Kalmiopsis* was first discovered and examined by botanists it was said to be most closely related to that delectable, if intractable little European alpine, *Rhodothamnus chamaecistus*. Unlike most *Ericaceae* in the wild, this tends to grow on limestone, though I find it more amenable to cultivation when grown in a well-drained, peaty, acid soil. Rarely more than 15cm high, *Rhodothamnus*, clothed in small, mid-green, elliptic leaves, sports a display of 3cm diameter, flat, clear pink blossoms. In another form, flowers are slightly smaller but with a tiny bright rose-red centre. Proof of its close relationship to *Kalmiopsis* came when introduction of pollen from the latter to the stigma of *Rhodothamnus* yielded good seed and subsequent seedlings. It was the red-eyed rhodothamnus

that was used in the cross and that feature is present in the seedlings. The habit owes more to *Rhodothamnus* than *Kalmiopsis* though plants differ from the former in their smaller flowers borne fewer to the raceme and in the lack of bristles on leaf margins. The hybrid is also easier to grow than its European parent.

A botanical name had to be found for the new hybrid and after several attempts and some help from Kew x *Kalmiothamnus ornithomma* was decided on. At one stage I had contrived to amalgamate both Latin and Greek in a name but was told quite firmly 'No, you can't do that' but eventually a specific name inspired by the red spot in the centre and meaning 'bird's eye' proved acceptable. Three of the seedlings were given cultivar names taken from nearby Devon tors, namely Cosdon, Hay Tor and Fox Tor, however, only the first two of these have made

X *KALMIOTHAMNUS ORNITHOMMA*

BARRY STARLING

it into the current *RHS Plant Finder*. Another hybrid, 'Sindelberg' originated on the continent and in this the clear pink *Rhodothamnus* was the seed parent so that the flowers of this hybrid lack the bird's eye. In all other respects it is very similar to my plants.

As long ago as 1845, a bigeneric hybrid between *Rhodothamnus* and *Phyllodoce empetriformis* was introduced as x *Phyllothamnus erectus*, and this neat little shrub has stood the test of time and is still valued by gardeners. Solitary, rose-pink flowers, broadly funnel-shape in form are held on 2cm long pedicels. These are clustered towards the tips of the shoots during April and, because they are sterile, remain in flower for a considerable time. Like so many of these small

X *PHYLLOTHAMNUS ERECTUS* (ABOVE)
X *PHYLLOTHAMNUS* 'CRINOLINES' *(BELOW)*

BARRY STARLING

Ericaceae it enjoys a little shade and shelter among adjacent shrubs of similar habit.

To the north of the Japanese island of Hokkaido stand the Daisetsu Mountains clothed on their summits by a variety of heath-like shrubs including two species of *Phyllodoce*, *P. caerulea* and *P. aleutica*, together with an incredible array of hybrids between those two species. In 1988 I obtained seed from this colony. One of the seedlings was particularly robust with large pink, egg-shaped flowers and this was to become the parent of a new x *Phyllothamnus*. One spring, as soon as *Rhodothamnus chamaecistus* opened its enchanting, pristine flowers, I approached it with pollen from the Daisetsu phyllodoce. The act I was about to commit seemed positively indecent – I knew that, once pollinated, that perfect flower would very quickly age and drop but nevertheless pollen was dabbed on the

PHYLLODOCE CAERULEA in Japan   BARRY STARLING

PHYLLODOCE (CAERULEA X ALEUTICA)
BARRY STARLING

outstretched stigma and the deed was done. In due course three strong, healthy seedlings were born of this union, developing into bushy, 20cm high plants with lustrous dark green foliage. Eventually, from close to the tips of shoots, purple buds on 4cm long red pedicels opened into crinoline-shaped flowers 1.25cm long and of equal width. Deep red calyces clasped rose-pink corollas at the waist with purple-black anthers protruding from the hem. Streaks of deeper pink followed pleats down the length of the flowers. In seeking a name for this new hybrid x *Phyllothamnus* 'Crinolines' seemed appropriate. Superficially, it resembles a larger version of x *Phylliopsis* 'Sugar Plum' but seems unaffected by *Phytophthora* when grown in pots or in the open ground.

And that concludes this account of this small group of bigenerics to date. Although 'Pinocchio', the first x *Phylliopsis* had as its seed parent *Kalmiopsis leachiana*, I had little success with crosses in that direction so have used phyllodoce species to bear the seed. All phyllodoce species appear to mate with *Kalmiopsis* with one exception: in spite of repeated attempts I cannot get the small, white flowered Japanese *P. nipponica* to accept *Kalmiopsis* pollen. There is still scope for more x *Phylliopsis* and x *Phyllothamnus* crosses but, no doubt, some will say 'why not leave the undeniably beautiful parent species alone? Stop trying to gild the lily.' Well, yes – I can see their point. But then variety is the spice of life!

X PHYLLOTHAMNUS 'CRINOLINES'
BARRY STARLING

Barry Starling

is a renowned alpine plant and Ericaceae *specialist, and a pioneering hybridiser, known particularly for his bi-generic crosses*

Showing rhododendrons – an amateur's perspective

RUSSELL BEESON

STAGING IN FULL SWING IN THE MARQUEE AT ROSEMOOR

RUSSELL BEESON

RHODODENDRON COMPETITIONS have a long tradition within the RHS. A key element of this was the often fierce rivalry between the major estate owners, dominated by the Rothschilds, the Loders, the Aberconways and others, as well as a number of famed private gardens of grand proportions with their many acres of sheltered woodland. Titles abounded, and the average gardener may well have felt that this was a game from which they were excluded. Nevertheless, we must be grateful for the magnificent contributions that these great gardens made to the shows, and still do to this day. The prize lists are still dominated, and rightly so, by gardens such as Exbury, Caerhays, Marwood Hill and a few others. Only they are able to produce the massive displays of the wide variety of species and hybrids that are needed to fill the exhibition hall. Indeed, without them there would be no show.

The main shows were, of course, always held in London, and so were dominated by those gardens willing and able to travel, often

significant distances, to the capital. Since the Main Rhododendron Competition moved to the RHS garden at Rosemoor in Devon, the make-up of the exhibitors has changed. Exbury are still able to make the journey, but we no longer see exhibits from the great gardens of southeast England. More entries now come from the southwest, particularly the wonderful Cornish gardens, which has changed the look of the show. If this competition were to be relocated to other parts of the country, the list of major exhibitors would naturally change once again as a result.

Having said all that, it is important to note the increasing contribution made to these shows by amateur gardeners, often with quite small gardens. For these exhibitors, the time-honoured question on the entry form requiring the 'gardener's name' is laughably inapplicable. We (and yes, I number myself amongst them) produce our exhibits by our own toil and sweat and often, to our great surprise and pleasure, are able to win prizes in full competition with

HOW EXBURY GARDEN TRANSPORT THEIR EXHIBITS   RUSSELL BEESON

the greatest gardens in the land. My purpose in this article is primarily to encourage other amateur gardeners to take part in these shows and to make some observations based on my own experiences over the last four years.

So why should a small-scale amateur gardener consider getting involved with the competitive showing of rhododendrons? I can only speak for myself, but I was persuaded by friends in the Rhododendron, Camellia and Magnolia Group that I should have a go and that it would above all be fun! I was sceptical at first, but decided to give it a try in 2009. It was hard work; it was a little intimidating; it was frustrating. But I have been back every year since because it was, as predicted, fun. Most importantly, I found that

HOW AMATEURS TRANSPORT THEIR EXHIBITS
RUSSELL BEESON

the camaraderie amongst the exhibitors turning up at 7.00 in the morning was infectious. As a relatively new member of the Group, and one who can hardly claim either to be an expert grower or to have a comprehensive collection, I found that participation in shows was a marvellous way of getting to know people of all backgrounds but with similar interests and dedication. Of course, one inevitable result of this has been a crash course in my education about rhododendrons.

The outlook of the small amateur grower is naturally rather different from that of the major exhibitor. The great gardens will often aim to enter as many classes as they can; winning the major cups remains an important

'EXBURY CORNER' IN THE MARQUEE AT ROSEMOOR   RUSSELL BEESON

competitive objective. The amateur is likely to be much more selective about the classes they will enter. Most amateurs cannot realistically hope to do well in the prestige classes for Six Species or Six Hybrids. The major estates will have many thousands of plants to select from and, most importantly, they will be taking much of their material from mature specimens whereas I, with my young garden, will often debate whether it is worth cutting off a significant portion of my immature shrub, just for a couple of days at the show. Even so, it is not unknown for amateurs to do well, even in these very challenging classes.

The major exhibitors have a huge job, with teams of gardeners picking their exhibits the day before the show, frequently working well into the night and often in bad weather; then

R. 'ALISON JOHNSTONE' (FIRST PRIZE TO RUSSELL BEESON, 2012)
RUSSELL BEESON/SALLY HAYWARD (*INSET*)

they have the equally onerous task of safely transporting their material to the show and staging the exhibits under great time pressure. The amateur can usually take a somewhat more leisurely approach, and be very choosy about his few exhibits. Sometimes, this can put the amateur at an advantage.

It is a fact that certain classes are often not well supported (particularly in the species section) and, although it might be called gamesmanship, the amateur would be well advised to get to know which these classes are and to consider whether they might be able to produce something for them. Not only will they be contributing to the interest and variety of the show, but they may also have a better chance of winning a prize.

Is it all about winning prizes? Of course not, though any exhibitor who denied the pleasure that prizes bring would, I think, be dishonest. A prize is recognition from the judges, always eminent experts in their field, as well as from one's peers and friends, that it has all been worthwhile. Contributing to the spectacle is very important as well. Often the pleasure comes from simply bringing along something of interest from your garden, knowing that you will be able to compare it with other exhibits and talk to experts and colleagues about it. Identification of unknown specimens is often a bonus. I have been both surprised and delighted to gain good numbers of prizes, including firsts, in every year

that I have taken part, as has my friend and close neighbour Robin Whiting, who started exhibiting at the same time as I did.

Moving on to some practical issues, for the Main Rhododendron Competition at Rosemoor, the South West branch of the Group (which is responsible for much of the organisation of the show) issues guidance notes to exhibitors regarding how to stage exhibits. These notes, written with new exhibitors in mind, are invaluable. Other authoritative advice on the whole subject of selecting, gathering, transporting and staging exhibits can be found, for example, in Peter Cox's book *The Larger Rhododendron Species*. Most of this advice is as applicable to the small amateur grower as it is to the great garden; often it is just a matter of scale. To illustrate this, compare the photographs showing how exhibits are transported, at one extreme, by Exbury Gardens and, at the other, by me.

SIX SPECIES (FIRST PRIZE TO EXBURY, 2011)
RUSSELL BEESON

KEY POINTS TO BEAR IN MIND
• Start planning several weeks in advance of the show. You will find it very difficult to decide what you are going to put in; it is a nail-biting time waiting to see what is and is not in flower for the show but remember that everyone is in the same position. Just enter for all the classes you think are possible. Late changes and additions can always be made, even on the day of the show.
• Study the Competition Schedule very carefully. A little creative thinking will enable one species

or variety to be exhibited in a number of different classes.

• Remember that you can enter as many exhibits as you want in any one class, so bring along everything you can find space for.

• Allow plenty of time for packing the car so that material remains fresh and doesn't fall over during the journey, and arrive as early as possible. Staging always takes longer than you imagine.

• The RHS supply vases (though in 2009, my first year, there was a serious shortage, which proved quite traumatic, resulting in exhibits being staged in jam jars and plastic milk bottles!)

• Bring along plenty of newspaper and moss for stuffing into the vases to hold exhibits steady.

• Bring secateurs, scissors and other tools for final manicuring of exhibits. You will be rightly marked down if your exhibit has faded flowers or dead twigs in evidence.

• Pay attention to the labelling of exhibits, as required by the Schedule.

AN AMATEUR (PAT BUCKNELL) COLLECTS THE LODER CUP FROM JIM GARDINER

SALLY HAYWARD

These days, colleagues and officials try their very best to help novice exhibitors, particularly in avoiding the dreaded 'NAS' (Not According to Schedule) card. As a new exhibitor, your knowledge of the botanical classification of rhododendrons will grow rapidly as you mull over which class a particular specimen belongs in.

I have tried to give you a flavour of what exhibiting is all about with the pictures included with this article. I do hope that some readers who may never have considered entering a show will be inspired to take the plunge. If you do, you will certainly improve your circle of friends and your knowledge of rhododendrons. Above all, you will also have a lot of fun!

JOHN ANDERSON OF EXBURY COLLECTS THE CROSFIELD CHALLENGE CUP FROM JOHN HILLIER

RUSSELL BEESON

Russell Beeson

is a retired Chartered Accountant, an amateur botanist and an active member of the New Forest and South West Branches of the Group

Paeonia and Wiener Schnitzel – the remarkable Dr Rock

CHARLES LYTE

HE WAS SHORT – FIVE FOOT, EIGHT INCHES – stocky, with a bit of a paunch, his hair was slicked down, and he peered from his slightly hooded eyes upon the world through rimless spectacles. If you had spared him a glance you would probably have concluded that he was a minor executive, a high street bank clerk, or perhaps an undertaker. He was Joseph Rock, plant hunter, and explorer, scholar, a man possessed of a towering intellect, and undoubted courage.

Joseph Rock was something of a fantasist, not averse to lying when necessary, a solitary man who suffered from mood swings, which included bursts of fury. He admitted that he had contemplated suicide. While he could be a highly entertaining dinner guest, particularly when he was given the uninterrupted opportunity to recount his adventures in China, where he collected prodigious quantities of seed, and herbarium specimens, he generally preferred his own company, and that of his servants and porters. While he enjoyed the company of women that is as far as it went; from an early age he made the decision to renounce sexual desire.

Botany and plant collecting were ideal occupations for him, providing the solitude he sought. As a collector he was meticulous. EHM Cox said that seed collected by Rock was sent to its destination cleaner, and with fewer rogues and a better percentage of germination, than from any other collector.

Rock was born in Vienna on January 13th, 1884. He was devoted to his mother, Franciska, and his grandmother, both of whom died when he was six years old, leaving him to be brought up by his father, Franz Rock, a poorly educated baker who became steward to a Polish nobleman, Count Potocki, who had a winter home in Vienna. Franz was a gloomy, dominating, religious maniac who made his wife's death the excuse for eccentric and morbid behaviour. Joseph was haunted by the memory of being made to put a flower between his mother's cold, stiff fingers as she lay in an open coffin, and throughout his childhood his father forced him to kneel and weep beside her grave. He went so far as to build an altar in his quarters, at which Joseph and his older sister, Karolina, had to act out the Mass daily. Franz was determined that Joseph would become a priest, Joseph was determined that he would not.

It is scarcely surprising that he was a sceptic and agnostic by choice, and had little liking for the missionaries he encountered on his expeditions, although he was amused by one, a

Joseph Brown, who led a sect called 'Brown's Salvationists', and whose letterhead bore the information – 'President – God, Vice-President - Jesus Christ, Treasurer – Joseph Brown.'

To counter the unhappiness of his childhood he used his imagination to construct a private world far from Austria and the increasingly weird behaviour of his father. As time passed, China became that fantasy world and at the age of thirteen he began to teach himself Chinese. He left school and home when he was eighteen, travelled around Europe scraping a living guiding tourists, or serving short spells as a seaman, despite the fact that he was suffering from incipient tuberculosis.

In 1905 he signed on as a cabin steward on the SS Zealand bound for New York. Eventually he made his way to Hawaii where he managed to get a job teaching Latin and natural history at Mills School, which became the Mid-Pacific Institute. He had learnt Latin in Vienna, but not at the University of Vienna, however, he convinced the still small Hawaiian academic community that he was a graduate of the University, and not only that he was qualified to teach Latin, but also botany, of which he had the scantiest knowledge. He must have had nerves of steel because he would spend his evenings boning up on botany so that he could teach his students the following day.

The botany deception was a defining moment in the turmoil of his life; in the first place he discovered a passion for the study of plants, and a great solace in the solitariness of field work. In certain ways he was very similar in temperament to another great Viennese botanist, Heinrich Handel-Mazzetti. Neither man suffered fools gladly, and both were capable of violence – Handel-Mazzetti was banned from the Natural History Museum in Vienna after attempting to hit the Director of the Botany Department – but when he and Rock met in Vienna in the winter of 1933–34 they were observed having a chummy meal at the Hotel Sacher. Obviously kindred souls. Peter Cox met him after the Second World War and found him blunt to the point of rudeness. 'I did not take to the man' he remarked after his visit to the Coxes' garden.

Rock's self-taught field work soon made him the leading authority on Hawaiian plants. He

BURMESE MEMBERS OF THE ROCK EXPEDITION IN THE CHAULMOOGRA FOREST
JOSEPH ROCK/ARNOLD ARBORETUM

was commissioned by the Board of Commissioners of Agriculture and Forestry to collect and document endemic Hawaiian plants, and in 1913 published *The Indigenous Trees of the Hawaiian Islands*, which for over seventy years remained the definitive work on the subject. He also became recognised as a thorough and successful agricultural collector, and in 1920 was sent to the Far East by the US Department of Agriculture to find and collect seed of the chaulmoogra, or kalaw, tree (*Hydnocarpus kurzii*), the source of chaulmoogra oil which was used successfully in the treating of leprosy.

The oil was imported from Indian bazaars, but because the demand outstripped the supply, the wild stands of the tree had to be found so that commercial plantations could be established. The first trees he found were not in fruit, but eventually he discovered a fruiting group and was able to gather a good harvest of seed. To make certain that he collected viable

RHODODENDRON RUFUM photographed by
Joseph Rock in June 1925, Koang-kei Shan, Gansu
JOSEPH ROCK/ARNOLD ARBORETUM

and successful seed he made further collections in Assam and Thailand. The multiple reaping of species was to mark all his future collecting, particularly of rhododendrons. He was meticulous to the point of being finicky. He was also commissioned by the USDA to find disease-free chestnuts. Chestnuts in America, where the bark was used in leather-tanning, had almost been wiped out by blight. He was successful in his search.

On Hawaii, Rock was well liked by the island society, and a popular and amusing dinner guest. But his conviviality and charm hid the dark mood changes that haunted him throughout his life. He wrote: *'In spite of all my friends, I was dreadfully lonely.'*

Although he appeared to feel his loneliness keenly, it was probably his inability to establish any truly close relationships that was the deepest hurt, and one, in a strange way, which was assuaged by his true love of the wilderness. Leading expeditions into often extremely dangerous areas in China he was not only in charge of his native collectors, porters and servants, which gave him the command and respect that had been denied him throughout his troubled childhood, but, perhaps more importantly, it gave him his self-respect. He never gave any hint of doubting himself, even if he must have at times.

During his expeditions he behaved more like a travelling potentate than his contemporary plant hunters, most of whom managed with relatively few servants, and with an austerity few modern travellers would relish. On one of his expeditions he had a caravan of thirty-three mules, and sixty yaks. His entourage included twenty armed and mounted men to protect the enterprise from bandits who terrorised the territory.

Included in the loads were the luxuries that Rock deemed essential. Every day servants were sent ahead to set up the night's camp site. The servants, cook, assistant cook, and butler would select a spot out of the worst of the weather, but with an agreeable view, and there the camp would be set up. The folding dining table would be placed on a leopard-skin rug, and laid with the fresh linen and clean napkins, and silver. Water was heated so that Rock could relax in his Abercrombie and Fitch folding bath before changing for dinner – Austrian dishes he had taught his chef to prepare – served on a camp table spread with a freshly laundered white linen cloth. His fastidiousness did not give way to roughing it in the wilds. Whenever he received even the most humble village headman, he was always impeccably dressed in a spotless white shirt, tie and jacket.

Rock also had a penchant for dressing up in native clothes, but only the finest. When he was living for a time in the then semi-independent kingdom of Choni, a remote district in the extreme south-west of Gansu, he was photographed in a kind of imperial pose dressed in a magnificent fur-trimmed silk brocade coat, an enormous fur hat, and decorated boots with up-turned toes. But when he posed with the Prince of Choni, who was wearing a far less elaborate costume, he wore

JOSEPH ROCK'S HERBARIUM SPECIMEN OF *RHODODENDRON ROCKII* R12064, collected in 1925 and subsequently reclassified as *Rhododendron hunnewellianum* ssp. *rockii*   ARNOLD ARBORETUM

A SELECTION OF JOSEPH ROCK'S RHODODENDRON COLLECTIONS
TOP ROW: RHODODENDRON CITRINIFLORUM R108, *R. CALOSTROTUM* SSP. *KELETICUM* R58
MIDDLE ROW: R. ADENOSUM R18228, *R. FORRESTII* R11169
BOTTOM ROW: R. TEMENIUM R114, *R. FLOCCIGERUM* TWO-TONED R10959

KEN COX/PAM HAYWARD/MIKE ROBINSON

European clothes, and looked for all the world like a Mr Pooter on his way to the station for the train to the City.

Rock's demand for perfection was not only a burden on his servants, but also upon himself. His herbarium specimens and bird skins were prepared with extraordinary care. This thoroughness extended to his seed collections of which he harvested prodigious quantities. Of a batch sent to the American Rhododendron Society it was said there was enough 'to plant the whole of Oregon'. Indeed so great was the surplus, which included primulas and meconopsis, as well as rhododendrons, that it was offered for sale to the public.

Despite his taste for style and luxury, as far as it was possible in the wilderness, Rock worked extremely hard, and endured considerable hardships. He dismissed danger and discomfort, and when he lectured on his expeditions he said he regarded them as 'perpetual picnics'.

Rock's transition from agricultural plant collector to an all-embracing collector took place in 1923 when he travelled in South-East Tibet and North-West Yunnan.

During that expedition he proved how industrious a collector he was. Apart from bird specimens and a range of plants, he returned with 609 rhododendron numbers, many of them the same species but from different plants and from different locations; there are no less than seventeen numbers for *Rhododendron crinigerum*, and while it was first collected and introduced in 1898, nevertheless the Rock collections of this species with flowers that range from white to rose pink are considered to be among the most attractive. He harvested thirteen numbers of *R. eclecteum*, which had already been introduced four years before. One of the most colour variable of the rhododendrons, Rock found his where there was a profusion of colour forms which gave enthusiasts a greater choice to select from.

Although Rock collected a prodigious amount of rhododendron seed from his expeditions to SE Tibet, and NW Yunnan, his introduction of new species was relatively small in number, which is probably why he is not rated among the great names of Forrest, Wilson and Kingdon-Ward, but his re-

introductions should be recognised for their valuable contribution to selection for cultivation and breeding.

As far as I can discover by combing through the Rhododendron Handbook, particularly the 1952 edition, he discovered and introduced *R. lanigerum* (R03913); *R. souliei* (also discovered by Wilson, Maire and McLaren); *R. rex*; *R. arizelum*; *R. vernicosum* aff (R03788); *R. adenosum*; *R. glischrum* ssp. *rude* 'Frank Kingdon-Ward' (R8228); *R. praestans* 'Sunte Rock' (R59480); *R. augustinii* ssp. *hardyi*; and *R. rigidum* – white form (R59207).

Undoubtedly, Joseph Rock is best known to gardeners for his beautiful *Paeonia rockii* (syn. *Paeonia suffruticosa* ssp. *rockii*), and *Sorbus* 'Joseph Rock', with its vibrant autumn colour and clusters of golden-yellow berries, but the sum total of his collecting must be recognised as an invaluable contribution to worldwide horticulture and agriculture. His photographic record of his expeditions is outstanding.

While China was created in his boyhood imagination as a magical place to escape to, it finally became the one place he wanted to live in and become part of, only to be taken from him through the revolution and the control of Communism.

JOSEPH ROCK, self-portrait taken in his study at Nguluko near Lijiang, Yunnan

A FURTHER SELECTION OF JOSEPH ROCK'S RHODODENDRON COLLECTIONS
TOP ROW: *RHODODENDRON CUNEATUM* R11392, *R. RACEMOSUM* 'ROCK ROSE' R11265
MIDDLE ROW: *R. FLETCHERIANUM* R22302, *R. ECLECTEUM* VAR. *ECLECTEUM* R23512
BOTTOM ROW: *R. STEWARTIANUM* R18376, *R. ECLECTEUM* VAR. *BELLATULUM* R11031

KEN COX/SALLY HAYWARD/MIKE ROBINSON

Rock's plant hunting was confined to just four expeditions (1923–1924 in South East Tibet and North West Yunnan; 1925–1926 in North West Gansu; 1929 and 1932, both in North West Yunnan) unlike the twenty-four that Frank Kingdon-Ward undertook, or George Forrest's seven, but he did make a considerable contribution to ornamental horticulture and research into the medical properties of Chinese and Tibetan flora.

Although he never entirely gave up plant hunting and collecting ornithological specimens, he began to take an increasing interest in the Nakhi people who had migrated from North-East Tibet to settle in the Likiang region.

MALUS ROCKII, first seen and collected by Joseph Rock in 1922 near Talifu, Yunnan at c.2500m; seen here in Yunnan, 2008 at c.3000m.
MIKE ROBINSON

They were completely unlike the Chinese, who regarded them as barbarians, being darker skinned, generally taller, well built, and good looking, clearly of Mongol origin, and said to have descended from Yeh-Yeh, a bastard son of Kublai Khan. According to their mythology their heroic ancestors had been hatched from eggs which were the product of the complicated copulation between mountains and lakes, pine trees and stones, and human women.

What fascinated Rock was the unique language of the Nakhi, which he learnt, while it was incomprehensible to the Chinese; their religion, which was a mixture of Tibetan pre-Buddha beliefs and shamanism, which they refused to give up, to the frustration of Christian Missionaries, who finally abandoned any attempt to convert them, and their use of two scripts – pictographic, similar in appearance to Egyptian hieroglyphics, and phonic script.

All their ancient religious writings were in pictographic script, which Rock was determined to master, and he did with the aid of Nakhi priest-sorcerers, and witch doctors, eventually producing a two volume dictionary. After initially being rejected, it was published in two volumes under the title of *The Ancient Na-Khi*

Kingdom of Southwest China; I did try to read it, but after becoming visually and cerebrally cross-eyed I admitted defeat about halfway through Volume One.

As his health deteriorated, so his bird and botanising expeditions in the Likiang countryside that he loved became fewer and shorter. His final dream was to die in his boyhood dreamland, but he was to be denied this when Mao Tse-tung led the Communists to victory over Chiang Kai-shek and his Nationalists.

In the summer of 1951 he left China for ever. He was 67, and died at 78 . His last eleven years have a great sadness about them; he could not settle, wandering in Europe and America, before finally settling and dying in Hawaii where his great China adventure had started.

Charles Lyte

is the biographer of Frank Kingdon-Ward and Sir Joseph Banks, and author of The Plant Hunters. In retirement, he is now attempting to restore a garden on the site of a long abandoned quarry in Devon

Managing a National Collection of magnolias

MARK FLANAGAN, JAIMIE PARSONS, TROY SCOTT SMITH and ALISON CLARKE
VAUGHAN GALLAVAN & MICHAEL KLEMPERER

AN APRIL VIEW OF VARIOUS CLONES OF *MAGNOLIA* X *LOEBNERI* IN THE VALLEY GARDENS, WINDSOR GREAT PARK. This image perfectly illustrates the value of multiple plantings and the use of Virginia Water lake as an 'eye catcher'   MARK FLANAGAN

MAGNOLIA GROWERS in the United Kingdom are fortunate in that they currently have access to five National Collections of the genus from which to draw inspiration and knowledge. Geographically well spread out, encompassing different soil types, landscapes and climates, and with individual circumstances of ownership and management, these collections offer a fascinating resource to the amateur.

The 1970s witnessed such dramatic changes in gardening styles in the United Kingdom that it was recognised there was a serious threat to the rich re-source of species and cultivars which had amassed in gardens over decades. Plant Heritage, formerly the National Council for the Conservation of Plants and Gardens (NCCPG) was set up in 1978 to address this. Taking a lead from botanic gardens who were developing approaches to the protection of threatened plants in the wild, this new organisation would have the conservation and propagation of endangered garden plants at its core. The National Collection Scheme is the principal vehicle through which this strategy is implemented – individuals or gardens favouring a particular genus, or even a single species and its cultivars, seek to assemble and maintain a taxonomically accurate, properly curated and documented collection which is then made available to the general public for educational purposes. There are now over 650 individual National Collections.

The custodians of the magnolia collections at Savill and Valley Gardens, Caerhays, Bodnant, Sherwood and Wentworth Castle have come together to share their experiences as National Collection Holders, not just with regard to the plants and associated practical matters but also to discuss the realities of the responsibility.

Magnolias in the Savill and Valley Gardens

MARK FLANAGAN

IT WAS EVIDENT from the earliest plantings in the Savill Garden that magnolias would find a congenial home in Windsor Great Park. Despite what several contemporary pundits perceived as adverse factors – low rainfall and low summer humidity and a hungry sandy soil – the first plantings succeeded splendidly. The exact date of these early plantings is difficult to pinpoint, though it is evident from the accounts written of this time, most importantly that of Lanning Roper[1] that these first plantings were made prior to the Second World War, the two notable specimens of *Magnolia* x *veitchii* 'Peter Veitch' are certainly of this vintage.

The pace of planting quickened with the return to the estate of demobilised staff and the appointment of master gardener Hope Findlay. Not only were the ravages of wartime neglect in the Savill Garden quickly put right but a whole new planting canvas became available with the decision, in 1946, to commence the clearance and opening up of the wooded areas on the north side of Virginia Water lake. Here the undulating topography, with views to the lake, and a framework of majestic broadleaved and coniferous trees offered a truly exceptional site for the creation of a woodland garden on the Royal scale.

Magnolias featured strongly in the early plantings including several seedlings received from CP Raffill at Kew in 1949. These seedlings, the result of a cross between *M. campbellii* and *M. campbellii* ssp. *mollicomata*, were planted at various locations. Other magnolias were purchased from the nursery trade, particularly Hilliers, or gifted from gardening friends. The smaller magnolias gave an almost immediate account of themselves, whilst the larger Yulania species and selections settled into a steady pattern of vegetative growth.

Excitement quickened in the autumn of 1958 when it was evident that one of Raffill's seedlings was carrying flower buds and the excitement reached a pitch the following spring when a number of sumptuous, bright purple-pink flowers emerged. It was named 'Charles Raffill' following the award of a preliminary commendation when shown at the RHS in 1961. Over time this tree has formed a wide-spreading individual with branches sweeping almost to the ground and is a well-known and celebrated specimen. One by one all the large-growing magnolias began to flower so that today's visitor can enjoy the prescience behind these inaugural plantings.

Magnolias continued to be planted in both gardens, accelerating with the promotion of John Bond to Keeper of the Gardens in 1975. John assiduously acquired magnolias from across the globe including representatives of newly released hybrids including those of Todd Gresham and Felix and Mark Jury. In 1982 the collection was registered with the National Council for the Conservation of

THE ORIGINAL TREE OF *MAGNOLIA* 'CHARLES RAFFILL' is one of the highlights of the Valley Gardens during favourable springs   MARK FLANAGAN

THE TRUE *MAGNOLIA SIEBOLDII* SSP. *SINENSIS,* estimably placed in a fold of Spring Wood in the Savill Garden   MARK FLANAGAN

Plants and Gardens (now Plant Heritage) as a National Collection and is now part of a unique genetic resource which also includes National Collections at four other gardens – Caerhays, Bodnant, Sherwood Garden and Wentworth Castle. In total the Windsor collection has in excess of 350 taxa with new plants added every winter.

With such a rich tradition of planting and cultivation what is our collective knowledge and experience of these wonderful flowering trees and shrubs? We are fortunate in having had a great deal of continuity of management of the gardens – only four men have overseen developments during a period of 80 years – with, in addition, long serving practical gardeners at the grass roots level. The traditions of excellence established by Sir Eric Savill are still the tenets that guide us today.

From a design perspective the importance of scale is vital. The Valley Gardens, in particular, now extending to over 200 acres, requires bold plantings in balance with their surroundings.

The tall tree-like magnolias can hold their own as individual specimens in such a landscape but medium to small growing forms need to be planted in numbers. All the M. x *soulangeana* hybrids are best presented as groups, a notable planting on the eastern edge of the Valley Gardens displays a large group of the strong growing 'Brozzonii', other groups extend along an attractive vista known as the Green Valley. Similarly, groups of the De Vos hybrids – aka the 'Eight Little Girls' – present a dynamic planting at the other end of the Valley Gardens in and amongst the *Rhododendron* species collection and illustrate a further point – magnolias are natural companions for other woodland subjects such as rhododendrons, camellias and Japanese maples.

The use of microclimates and topography should be carefully considered. Both the Savill and Valley Gardens benefit from a canopy of high-pruned oaks, sweet chestnuts and Scots pines which provide shelter from wind, strong summer sunshine and, to some extent, damaging spring frosts. The phenomenon of cold air sinking to the lowest point in the landscape is very evident in the Valley Gardens and its recognition has resulted in some conscious actions. Setting plants on the higher slopes, if only by a few metres, can make all the difference to a tender species or the flowers of a magnolia during a spring frost, certainly frost pockets need to be identified and avoided.

Careful placement is also a factor in making the best use of the ornamental qualities of magnolias. The aforementioned *Magnolia campbellii* (Raffillii Group) 'Charles Raffill' enjoys an open aspect, though sheltered from the southwest, allowing it to be seen from some distance – a magnificent beacon of colour on a gloomy March or April day. Throughout the Valley Gardens huge magnolias can be viewed from above, on a level and below, all carefully placed for maximum effect, thus making intelligent use of the topography. Equally, concealing and revealing smaller magnolias can be an effective ploy. In Spring Wood in the Savill Garden several magnolias reveal themselves to an unsuspecting visitor as they walk the winding paths; many times I have seen excited groups of people enjoying a particularly well-placed specimen of M. *sieboldii* ssp. *sinensis*.

***MAGNOLIA* X *KEWENSIS* 'WADA'S MEMORY'** is a plant gaining in approbation; it's unique qualities are evident in this image of a young tree at Frogmore in the Home Park at Windsor   MARK FLANAGAN

THE MAIN VALLEY IN LATE MARCH where Hope Findlay's magnolia plantings from the late 1940s are now magnificently mature

MARK FLANAGAN

PRACTICALITIES & PROBLEMS

Good planting technique is a must and should go without comment. However, it is not always followed and corners are cut. Two points need to be made. Magnolias have fleshy roots which are easily damaged and extra care must be taken at planting time. Planting depth is vital; so many trees are planted too deep and yet it is so easy to get this right, simply measure the depth of the hole against the root ball of the plant to ensure that the stem/root junction sits just at the soil surface.

If you are lucky enough to garden in a rabbit and deer-free environment, I envy you. If not, then protection from browsing is vital. Ensure that the materials used are up to the job and the size and height of the guard is adequate. Also remember that magnolias have thin bark, even as large established specimens, and may need to be protected from rabbits, in particular, for an extended period of time – a 12m specimen of *M. dawsoniana*, perhaps 60 years old, was ring-barked by rabbits browsing in the Valley Gardens during the hard winter of 2009/10. Each site will have its own suite of pests, the knowledge of which is vital to ensure the survival and establishment of your precious plants. Slugs, for example, can be a major pest

in certain situations and pose a real threat to seedlings in the propagation stage or young saplings when first set out.

Another common failure is to neglect watering of newly planted stock. In all but the wettest springs irrigation will be needed to ensure successful establishment. Controlling weed growth on and around young plants is also good, basic husbandry. Where possible, bed planting is much better than 'pot' planting a magnolia into a strong growing grass sward.

In the Savill and Valley Gardens we do not routinely feed our magnolias, the rich woodland soils, built up over hundreds of years, provide a nutritious and well balanced substrate. However, there is no doubt that young plants can be encouraged by the application of fertiliser and there are now proprietary products available. Nitrogen-rich fertilisers will provide a boost to growth in the spring, whilst a high potash mixture will assist in the ripening of wood and the production of flowers when applied in late summer. Mulching with organic matter is akin to a religion at Windsor and the shallow roots of magnolias clearly enjoy generous treatment. Leaf mould is still the best substance for this purpose and is to be recommended. However, we generate large quantities of 'lop and top' and when properly composted this produces very acceptable woody mulch which is now our staple mixture for surface applications.

Finally, the vexed question of formative pruning. Many advocate no pruning at all and a plausible case can be made for such an approach. In my experience, however, magnolias are untidy growers in their early years often producing masses of shoots in all directions which make for poorly shaped mature trees. I would always wish to employ formative pruning for the long-term benefit of the plant but would make a plea to be clear about what you are trying to achieve and to fully understand the plant in question. Many magnolias are naturally shrubby and do not need to be pruned to a single stem. Of those that are tree-like the maintenance of apical dominance, with an obvious strong-growing leading shoot, will not only produce shapely and beautiful trees but will avoid structural defects developing, such as split leaders, that may fail catastrophically in the mature specimen. A gradual lifting of the canopy will accommodate the cultivation of an understorey of companion plants but is not obligatory and low branches do allow a close up view of flowers. I prefer to prune in winter when the framework of deciduous species can be seen and time is available to do a proper job, but don't leave it too late, the sap often begins to rise surprisingly early in the New Year. Routine pruning of established trees and shrubs should not be necessary but can be done, for example, where a specimen has outgrown its available space and, in this case, summer pruning will avoid the loss of spring flowers.

FAVOURITE PLANTS

Magnolias are generally easy, long-lived plants that increase in beauty each and every year and fully reward any effort made on their behalf. The question of personal favourites is a difficult one, with so many beautiful plants to choose from it is almost impossible to hone the list down to a chosen few, and the list will change over time as recently planted cultivars assert their beauty and old favourites remind us of their charms. However, my current top five are as follows –

Magnolia 'Spectrum' – The Mulan (*Magnolia liliiflora*) – has been a generous and influential parent in hybridisation programmes. Breeders have been attracted by several well-marked characters in this Chinese species. It blooms over an extended period of time, with flowers that exhibit a degree of frost hardiness and has proved a fertile parent. Its flowers are narrow and upright and immediately recognisable and this floral form is carried through into its progeny allowing its presence to be perceived even when the hybrid may be unfamiliar. I have a soft spot for the hybrids from *M. liliiflora* and could easily have picked any one of the many, including several of Todd Gresham's 'Svelte Brunettes' such as 'Heaven Scent' or 'Peppermint Stick' or Os Blumhardt's first-class 'Star Wars' however, I always greatly admire the flowering of *M.* 'Spectrum' a hybrid raised by William Kosar, a horticulturist at the US National Arboretum. A specimen in the Valley

MAGNOLIA X SOULANGEANA 'PICKARD'S SCHMETTERLING' inherits the large, beautifully formed flowers of 'Picture' but has even more vivid coloration on the outside of the tepals

MARK FLANAGAN

MAGNOLIA 'ERIC SAVILL' – GORGEOUS!
HARVEY STEPHENS

Gardens has now reached 6–7m in height with a spread of perhaps 5m. It is a mid-season plant with us, generally appearing in early to mid-April and for a 4–5 week period before the last of the flowers are lost within the emerging foliage. The flowers themselves are poised beautifully amongst the branches, narrow and erect and reddish purple on the outside, paler within. A sister seedling – 'Galaxy' is barely less fine, though with slightly smaller flowers.

Magnolia 'Wada's Memory' intrigues me. As magnolias go it isn't classically beautiful, indeed the floppy nature of its flowers, a day or so after opening may be regarded as a negative quality. But herein lies the intrigue because the effect of this phenomenon is to give the plant a quite unique appearance that is totally arresting. When seen from a distance the plant appears to have been hung with a myriad of strips of white cloth which are no less startling at close quarters. All our plants are developing into upright specimens with a noticeably elongated pyramidal outline. The great Koichiro Wada is well served by association with this singular magnolia.

Magnolia 'Pickard's Schmetterling' – we also have Mr Wada to thank, by association, for this cultivar as it derives from an open-pollinated plant of 'Picture' which is a clone introduced from Wada's Yokohama Nursery before the Second World War. The cross occurred in the Canterbury gardens of Amos Pickard and the resultant plant has flowers which are produced in great profusion and with a scintillating quality found in few other forms of *M.* x *soulangeana*. Although I'm not sure I see any butterflies!

Magnolia 'Caerhays Belle' – once seen, never forgotten is the only apt phrase for the magnificent original tree planted against the ramparts at Caerhays Castle. I was fortunate enough to see this specimen at its absolute peak in March 2009 when innumerable flowers were set against a blue watercolour-wash sky. The cross uses two of China's finest – *M. sargentiana* var. *robusta* and *M. sprengeri* 'Diva' – and maintains its blue chip credentials with large flowers of a distinctive salmon pink that incline to the side in a coquettish way worthy of its name.

Finally, it would be remiss of me not to pick *Magnolia* 'Eric Savill'. This is a very good magnolia, a Caerhays seedling of *M. sprengeri* 'Diva', with flowers of a radiant rich pink held jauntily along the pendent secondary branches in April. Its association with the Windsor 'dream team' – it was planted by Hope Findlay and named by John Bond for Sir Eric Savill – only adds to its lustre. The flowering of the original tree in the Savill Garden is much anticipated and in recent years it has rarely let us down.

REFERENCE ■ 1. Roper, Lanning. *The Gardens in the Royal Park at Windsor*, Chatto and Windus, (1959).

Mark Flanagan

is Keeper of the Gardens in Windsor Great Park

Magnolias at Caerhays

JAIMIE PARSONS

MAGNOLIA STELLATA, the first magnolia to arrive at Caerhays, in 1887, and still performing

JAIMIE PARSONS

AT THE OUTSET, the main interest of the founder of the garden at Caerhays Castle, John Charles (JC) Williams, lay with daffodils, camellias and bamboos. The first magnolia to arrive came in 1887 and was, in fact, *Magnolia stellata*. It was planted outside the nursery window and, despite having been cut back several times, and regularly having to be cut back away from the window, it survives today. The next magnolia event to attract JC Williams' attention was the article written by George Nicholson in the first issue of *Flora and Sylva* which appeared in April 1903. This publication was edited by the great William Robinson, and its first colour plate is a reproduction of a painting of two open blooms of *M. x soulangeana* 'Rustica Rubra' from his garden, Gravetye Manor. Nicholson provided a list of magnolias growing in the British Isles at that time and it was from this article that JC Williams' interest in magnolias was born.

JC Williams was the sole sponsor of George Forrest's third Chinese expedition between 1912–1915, at a time when the principal new plant introductions were from the genus *Primula*. In his paper to the Primula Conference held on April 16th 1912, Professor Bayley Balfour wrote *'Forrest is again in Yunnan collecting*

MAGNOLIA FLORIBUNDA F17809, introduced to Caerhays in the 1920s   JAIMIE PARSONS

The first new magnolia to arrive came under collection number F24214 *Magnolia mollicomata* which was soon diagnosed as *M. campbellii* ssp. *mollicomata*. We have at least three magnolias in the garden growing under this number and three more of the same species but with no number attached.

Another deciduous magnolia in the collection is *M. rostrata* (F24827), grown from seed collected at the same time but now, sadly, barely alive.

M. nitida came to Caerhays under two Forrest numbers: F26509 collected along the Burma/Salween divide in April 1925 and F26381, which may well be among the collection but to date no label has been found.

An earlier Forrest collection, but not introduced to the garden until the 1920s, is *Michelia floribunda* F17809 (now *Magnolia floribunda*), described in the field notes as having fragrant flowers of a creamy yellow and found in mixed forests in April 1919 on the Schweli/Salween divide.

HYBRIDS AT CAERHAYS

One needs to be a very patient gardener if growing the tree magnolias. I can remember when my predecessor, the late Philip Tregunna, told me that they had to wait for 40 years before *Magnolia campbellii* flowered, and many grown on their own rootstock can take years to flower in our climate. Philip showed me that day how to hybridize, although unfortunately none of my magnolias took in that year, and it was not until the year 2000 that my first pollination was successful. However, that was just the beginning – we then had to get past the vermin – from the squirrels, mice, rabbits and now deer –and of course growing these plants in a woodland garden, there is always the chance of windblown or fallen trees that can take out a newly planted area or a mature magnolia.

We have made many a hybrid since then at Caerhays and learned the lessons! You have to have the perfect day: the pollen has to be ripe and ready, as does the flower that receives it. A few more perfect days are needed afterwards, and then a good take and germination rate, and then you will need the room to grow the seedlings on. So the message is: choose your hybridizing partners carefully.

for JCW of Caerhays Castle.' JC went on to jointly sponsor all of Forrest's later expeditions and by the time of the 1924 collecting trip his attention had moved on to include other species, especially evergreen trees and magnolias.

MAGNOLIA HYBRID JP20, raised by the author, is being trialled at Caerhays before naming

JAIMIE PARSONS

Once our hybrids flower, we give them two to four years to prove themselves and if the flower is consistently good, then we will grow on. However, if it does not perform as expected, then we will cut it down and dig out the roots, as we need the room.

PRACTICALITIES & PROBLEMS

One of the many problems we face at Caerhays is rabbits ring barking our young magnolias, and in some hard winters they will also go for older, even fully mature plants. We place chicken wire around as soon as we plant, using small stakes to keep the wire in place, along with a spiral guard. Do look inside the spiral after a while, as we have had ants build their nests up inside them and the plant dying because of this. Spirals should also be checked from time to time for expansion, as some do not unroll as they should. Of course, another form of control is to resort to the gun, but watch out you don't miss the rabbit and hit the magnolia!

Deer are also becoming a problem, shooting them is an option not open to all, so consider using taller wire and erecting this further from the plant.

Damage from slugs and snails in 2012 was the worst ever experienced because of the extraordinarily wet weather, although it proved a great growing season for the same reason. We slug baited around all our magnolias which are 6ft and under on three occasions during the year, but even so one or two were still completely stripped of their leaves. Seedlings take a bashing from them too, so it pays to be really vigilant.

Squirrels are also a problem, not only to magnolias but to most of the other plants within the gardens; baiting these too has been a great success. Information on this can be found via the Forestry Commission in the UK, but it is not a cheap method.

Mice can cause havoc when sowing magnolia seed – they go for them like children let loose in a sweet shop! To get around this, we sow our seed around November in pots, and cover with glass to keep the mice out, leaving the top of the compost, once the seed is sown, about two inches below the top of the pot, so when they start to germinate around April, they don't hit the glass straight away.

Mice have also been known to nibble at the base of our plants in the standing beds during the winter months and this needs watching out for.

Grafted plants have given us concern over the years: some of them appear not to want to grow upright, they flop over, and so a lot of otherwise unnecessary staking has had to take place, and of course then you have to keep an eye on the tree ties.

A minority of the visiting public can also bring problems, from stealing cuttings to taking seed that is not ripe thus snapping off branches, or removing labels, even labels that are nailed to posts, and on a couple of occasions flowers have been taken for their pollen.

MAGNOLIA CAMPBELLII 'ALBA', pristine and the perfect foil to the bright coloured varieties

JAIMIE PARSONS

MAGNOLIA **'CAERHAYS BELLE'** – once seen, never forgotten   MARK FLANAGAN

Magnolia 'JC Williams' FCC a cross made by Philip Tregunna, the pollen parent was *M. sprengeri* 'Diva' seedling x first generation seedling of *M. sargentiana* var. *robusta*. An important magnolia because of the shape of its flower which is subtly different to that of *M. campbellii* ssp. *mollicomata* var. 'Lanarth'. Named after JC Williams, creator of the garden who purchased the original *M. sprengeri* 'Diva' and was one of the first to flower *M. sargentiana* var. *robusta* in the UK.

Magnolia 'Caerhays Belle' FCC (*sargentiana* var. *robusta* x *sprengeri*) Bred by Head Gardener Charles Michael in 1951, it took 14 years to flower.

Magnolia 'Caerhays Surprise' AM, CORY CUP 1973 (*campbellii* ssp. *mollicomata* x *liliiflora* 'Nigra') Bred by Philip Tregunna in 1959.

Magnolia 'FJ Williams' FCC (*sargentiana* var. *robusta* x *campbellii* ssp. *mollicomata* 'Lanarth') Planted in 1987, registered and named 2009.

Magnolia 'Delia Williams' FCC (*sargentiana* var. *robusta* x *campbellii* ssp. *mollicomata*) Planted in 1972, named after the wife of FJ Williams and registered in 2009.

Press – friend or foe? While we all hope the Press will talk about our gardens in the local papers to encourage the public to visit, they can get it wrong. A good example of this would be saying that after a frost all the gardens are ruined, but not every garden suffers, and of course there is so much more to come out in a day or two. A chance and thoughtless statement in a newspaper can quickly impact on visitor numbers.

I have also noticed that particular indicators of how the season has been will determine the quality of the flowers the following year: with no seed, good growth and plenty of sun to ripen the wood, we have found that the colour of the flower is better, but with lots of seed, poor growth and no sun to ripen the wood, the flower quality is not so good the following year, but I'm sure I will be proven wrong in this theory!

FAVOURITE PLANTS

Of all the magnolias in the garden, I think it is the Caerhays hybrids that the public and great gardeners come to see and talk about. The first three are particular favourites of mine.

MAGNOLIA **'CAERHAYS SURPRISE'**, one of the most successful of the new varieties

JAIMIE PARSONS

THE PLANTING AT CAERHAYS DEMONSTRATES HOW MAGNOLIAS BLEND PERFECTLY WITH CAMELLIAS AND OTHER TREES AND SHRUBS

JAIMIE PARSONS

Magnolia 'Philip Tregunna' FCC (*sargentiana* var. *robusta* x *campbellii*) First flowered in 1968, named and bred by Philip Tregunna, Head Gardener 1956–1996.

Magnolia 'Burncoose' AM (A seedling of *M. sprengeri* 'Diva') Raised by Arnold Dance, Head Gardener at Burncoose, it first flowered in 1972.

Two other magnolias I would personally hate to miss each year are *M.* 'Betty Jessel' and *M. campbellii* 'Alba', the first for its fabulous colour and huge flowers and the second for the its purity and the contrast it brings to the display. The first yellow magnolia, *M.* 'Elizabeth', came to Caerhays in the 1980s. Since then we have planted many more including 'Gold Star', 'Yellow Fever', 'Yellow Bird', 'Yellow Lantern', 'Sundance'. They have certainly extended the flowering period of magnolias within the gardens, yet some I feel are a wish-wash colour and need to be planted against a dark hedge/ background. The one that does stand out to date is *M.* 'Daphne'.

Also extending the flower season is *Magnolia* 'Yuchelia' ('Miss Honeybee' x *figo*), the flower of this plant has the scent of a michelia and pink petals which have flashes of green on the outside, pinky-white on the inside, a 'must have' for the collectors.

Caerhays was awarded National Magnolia collection status in 2001, much deserved after all the work the family and staff have put in over the generations. If it were not for the constancy of the Williams family's investment that has been ploughed into these gardens, in both time and money, together with the staff's passion in their work, we would not have these wonderful gardens. This is true of all the other great gardens we have the pleasure of visiting but we must be careful not to forget that we are all just custodians for the next generation, to allow them to put their mark on and follow us in the history books.

Finally, with a great garden or National Collection, comes the inevitable paperwork and we must not get too buried in it; make time to get out into the garden, take notes and photographs and keep on learning.

Jaimie Parsons

is Head Gardener at Caerhays Castle Gardens in Cornwall

Magnolias at Bodnant

ALISON CLARKE & TROY SCOTT SMITH

MAGNOLIA DENUDATA SEEN FROM THE HOUSE AT BODNANT

ALISON CLARKE

BODNANT GARDEN IS SITUATED above the River Conwy on ground sloping towards the west, and looks across the valley towards the Snowdon range. In addition to the fine views of river and mountains, it has the advantages of abundant running water and a background of large native trees, many of them planted about 1792. In spring, a carpet of narcissi spills down the valley sides heralding the awakening season. The effect is magical and the memory will be etched long in your mind. Chasing these narcissi into flower are a host of other spring delights, none more spectacular than the magnolias, for which Bodnant is justly famous.

The McLaren family financially contributed towards plant hunting expeditions in the early 1900s and Bodnant Garden also benefited from other collectors, notably George Forrest, Frank Kingdon-Ward and Dr Joseph Rock, who sent home hundreds of new species, many of which are still grown here today.

The first magnolias were planted at Bodnant during the early years of the last century. These were mainly *Magnolia campbellii, M. sprengeri* and *M. sargentiana* var. *robusta*, many of these thought to have been raised from seed collected by the aforementioned collectors. These varieties all flower early in the season, typically the end of February into early March and when there is a mild spring (as in 2012) the flowers put on a dramatic display. In other years one or two nights of sharp hard frosts can reduce them to a sad brown mush, sometimes just as the eagerly anticipated flowers are breaking bud. In 2011 the very cold weather at the beginning of the year caused these magnolias to keep their buds tightly shut until at least a month later than usual. When they did finally open, the result was one of the best flower displays that we have had from these plants in living memory.

As the garden developed, large numbers of later flowering species were added, such as

Magnolia salicifolia, which is a real favourite amongst everyone here and greatly admired for its simple, elegant beauty. *Magnolia denudata* was also widely planted, especially in the areas near to the house, and in particular, an avenue of these along the Tennis Lawn puts on a truly impressive display every April. These later varieties generally escape severe frosts and so provide a longer lasting and more reliable display of flowers. Many of the best specimens of magnolia in the garden are planted below the lowest Terrace in an area known as the Magnolia Walk.

MAGNOLIA SARGENTIANA **VAR.** *ROBUSTA*   ALISON CLARKE

The biggest magnolias at Bodnant are *Magnolia* x *veitchii* 'Peter Veitch' of which there are several massive and venerable specimens, all thought to date from approximately 1908 and probably purchased from Veitch Nursery when they closed. It is known that Bodnant bought up a huge consignment of plants from them at that time.

The climate and soil conditions are somewhat of a mixed bag as far as growing magnolias is concerned. The rainfall averages some 43 inches, or 1090mm, a year, but we have also suffered drought conditions, especially in 1976, when many plants were lost. The soil at Bodnant Garden is a stiff boulder-clay, overlying a friable shaly rock; in places the former has been denuded, and there the soil is lighter. The garden fortunately has no lime in it, though there is limestone four or five miles away. It has a great deal of clay, but luckily it occurs on the slope and so is well drained.

There is a great deal of wind from the southwest, but the wind from that direction is mild and moist and does not do much harm. There is frost, about the same as you get all round the south and north of London. It is not a mild climate because although the beneficent Gulf Stream flows up along the western coast of Wales, there is a great and regrettably placed island called Anglesey which interrupts this movement of air, and directs it up to Scotland instead of allowing it to flow round to the Conwy River.

The walls of the terraces at Bodnant were used to good effect to provide shelter for many tender and borderline hardy plants including evergreen magnolia species such as *Magnolia grandiflora* (the cultivar 'Goliath' being planted in numerous spots).

MAGNOLIA SALICIFOLIA   ALISON CLARKE

MAGNOLIA WILSONII   ALISON CLARKE

newly purchased specimens. Something that we observed for the first time last year is the phenomenon of squirrels 'eating' flower buds. They could be clearly seen pulling off flower buds that were at the point of opening, they would then take just one bite, at the base of the bud and discard it. We are not quite sure why they do this, and can only guess that they are possibly draining out nectar from the base of the bud, but whatever the reason, it is utterly infuriating to watch.

The National Collection of Magnolia Species at Bodnant is a long-standing one, first registered at the very beginning of Plant Heritage (or the NCCPG as it was then). This poses us some problems, as there is nobody working here currently that has the kind of in-depth knowledge of a genus that develops when you are the person that has initiated and built up a particular collection. It is always hard when you 'inherit' a collection (as is so often the case in large public gardens), you are thrown in at the deep end, looking after a varied and extensive collection without time to first learn how best to cultivate and propagate those plants.

M. delavayi – sadly one of our oldest specimens (100 years old) succumbed to the recent devastatingly low temperatures in the winter of 2010/2011. Temperatures plummeted with –17°C recorded on one night, they then hovered around or below –8°C for the best part of two weeks. Another *M. delavayi*, thought to be of a similar age was cut hard to the ground and initially also appeared to be dead, but this spring, after doing nothing for a year, it started throwing out healthy young shoots from the base. Many of our more tender evergreens have suffered a similar fate and have had to 'start again'. Looking back into records from the past, it appears that this may well be the third time that some of the older evergreens have been cut to the ground, the same thing having happened in the winters of 1947 and 1963 respectively.

PRACTICALITIES & PROBLEMS

We find that our main pest problem is rabbits ring barking plants; just what so attracts them to magnolia bark totally eludes us, but they have even gone as far as digging their way under and up into our quarantine tunnel to get at our

MAGNOLIA DELAVAYI   ALISON CLARKE

PART OF THE MAGNOLIA COLLECTION SEEN FROM THE TENNIS LAWN   ALISON CLARKE

Also you don't have the time to devote to studying one genus when there are other collections or important groups of plants within the garden that are of equal importance to the garden as a whole. This has very much been our experience at Bodnant.

Many of our existing plants are now very old and they are slowly dying back and getting a 'stag's horn' appearance, so there is an urgent need to replace them, however, we have found it particularly hard to purchase good and sizeable specimens of most of the species mentioned at the beginning of this article.

Due to the difficulties in buying the plants that we need, we have decided to try to propagate some ourselves. It has been very many years since magnolias were propagated here at Bodnant either commercially (for sale at Bodnant Garden Nursery) or for use in the garden. Initially we hope to try growing plants from seed and to this end we have recently acquired some seed from the Group seed exchange, which is germinating well. We are also collecting and sowing some of our own seed, and would be grateful for any tips and advice on this subject from other members of the Group.

Alison Clarke

is Propagator and Taxonomist at Bodnant

Troy Scott Smith

is Head Gardener at Bodnant Garden

Magnolias at Sherwood

VAUGHAN GALLAVAN

A CLASSIC SHERWOOD SCENE WHERE NATURALISTIC PLANTING, INSPIRED BY ITS BEAUTIFUL SURROUNDINGS, LENDS ITSELF PERFECTLY TO THE DISPLAY OF MAGNOLIAS

VAUGHAN GALLAVAN

WHILE THE WINTRY OAK RESTS in bare twigged bud, snowdrops fade and daffodils push through banks of dormant grasses, other naked branches show hints of the vivid colour that is to follow. The precocious emergence of magnolia flowers is surely one of the most beautifully dramatic shows in nature and in our gardens. Precarious in our unpredictable oceanic Spring weather and sometimes fleeting, the early flowering magnolias are definitely a risk worth taking.

In the late 1960s, when the Quicke family moved to Sherwood, the only magnolias in the garden were three specimens of *Magnolia* x *soulangeana*, two similar to 'Rustica Rubra' and one 'Alexandrina Alba'. These 80 year old trees

flower reliably and are rarely damaged by frost. Over the following thirteen years another twenty or so hybrids and species were added. Subsequent years have seen the collection expand to more than 270 plants. It is over this last 31 years that I have been engaged with the management, expansion and development of the garden and of its three National Collections of which *Magnolia* is the most impressive.

A passion for magnolias inspired the late Sir John Quicke to include these wonderful trees in the already diversely planted Sherwood site. Initial stock comprised plants from the Veitch and Hillier nurseries and layers from the Newton St. Cyres Arboretum, where the

Quickes had first started gardening. As a mark of their resilience, eighteen magnolias have survived 40 years of neglect at the Arboretum, which is currently under restoration.

Other plants came as gifts, notably *M. campbellii* ssp. *mollicomata* from Sidbury and an open pollinated seedling from Killerton of *M. dawsoniana*. The latter took 28 years to bloom and was under threat of removal before emerging as one of the 'stars' of the garden. This long period from seedling to flowering is not unusual. Also present in the earlier plantings were *M. denudata*, *M. salicifolia*, *M. liliiflora* 'Nigra', 'Merrill', *M. kobus* var. *borealis*, *M.* x *soulangeana*, 'Alba Superba' and 'Lennei Alba', all very fine plants.

Sherwood falls in the rain shadow of Dartmoor and has an average annual rainfall of 30 inches. At 400 feet above sea level it is far colder than the Cornish gardens and flowering is at least two weeks later than most there. Nearly every year I am able to enjoy a double magnolia season by making an early 'pilgrimage' to Caerhays. We have experienced temperatures below –13°C and, in recent winters, prolonged frosts have been sufficient to cause root damage to young stock.

Spanning two steep sided, north facing valleys, cut through Culm Measure Clay and protected by ancient oak woodland, the site has been favourable for the cultivation of magnolias but not without problems. The steep ground is ideal for enjoying the blooms from above and below but frost has been damaging in the lower areas. Heeding initial mistakes we've tended to plant early flowering trees at the top of the garden. While one *Magnolia campbellii* 'Alba' is resplendent, another in the lower valley is sometimes so badly frosted that no buds open. Frost seems to be more problematic following mild weather in January and February. During persistently cold winters the buds tend to remain fully closed and the flowers are unblemished. *Magnolia campbellii* acquired from the Veitch nursery in 1969 has rarely made a good display. It tends to bud prolifically in alternate years but these often coincide with the mild late winter conditions previously described. However on the few occasions that it has flowered, it is magnificent and hence has thus far been spared its place.

A prolonged cold winter moving to a warm, frost-free spring has produced the best of displays with an almost simultaneous flowering of the earlier plants. These conditions are not trouble-free, however, as we have then suffered the loss of young grafted plants, the grafts apparently failing under the pressure of a sudden burst of growth.

I have to admit to a liking for most of the magnolia flowers that I've seen, including those that are more curiosities than blooms of great beauty. The magnolia trees and shrubs blend seamlessly with the native trees which form the background of our site. They also compliment the exotic broadleaved and coniferous introductions and are natural companions to many species of *Rhododendron*. I find the question of personal favourites a challenge and also don't know that my tastes will help inform other people's choices.

There are, however, many first class plants that I have liked from first sight and some more recent introductions to this collection that are worthy of note. I regard with envy some splendid specimens in other collections: *M. sprengeri* var. *sprengeri* 'Diva' at Caerhays, the giant *M. campbellii* in Rosemary Howell's garden, Lukesland, and 'Marwood Spring' at Marwood Hill to mention but three.

Apart from its propensity to frost damage by virtue of early flowering, *M. denudata* is a perfect plant, with superb flower form, scent and colour. It has parented a wide range of fine hybrids,

MAGNOLIA 'ANNE ROSSE' SHOULD BE MORE WIDELY GROWN   VAUGHAN GALLAVAN

many of which are represented in the Sherwood collection: M. x *soulangeana* 'Pickard's Sundew' and 'Pickard's Schmetterling' are both wonderful plants; M. 'Anne Rosse', a hybrid with M. *sargentiana* var. *robusta* ought to be more widely grown and M. x *soulangeana* 'Lennei Alba', an important descendent of M. *denudata*, was used by Todd Gresham to produce a spectacular group of hybrids. I often hear people say that there are too many Gresham hybrids but there are few here that I would want to lose. 'Manchu Fan' retains the fine qualities of M. *denudata* but flowers a good month later and is rarely frosted. 'Raspberry Ice' guarantees an amazing show every April. The large blooms of 'Phelan Bright' may offer consolation for those unable to grow M. *campbellii*. Perhaps there is something to be said for restraint in naming too many similar hybrids. I like the de Vos and Kosar eight 'Little Girls' but don't know that they all deserve Awards of Garden Merit. 'George Henry Kern' is the same cross but significantly different in flower colour, duration of blooming and has a dwarf habit. This is the slowest and lowest growing magnolia in the Sherwood collection and definitely worth considering for smaller gardens.

The Jury hybrids feature widely at Sherwood and are some of my personal favourites. M. 'Lennei Alba' is also a constituent of the beautiful 'Athene', 'Milky Way' and the splendid but not so widely grown 'Lotus'. 'Apollo' is frequently requested by

DARK AND SHAPELY *MAGNOLIA* 'BETTY JESSEL' IS WELL COMPLEMENTED BY AN EQUALLY LOVELY 'CAERHAYS BELLE' SEEDLING   VAUGHAN GALLAVAN

visitors to my plant sales. I recommend this as a large flowered tree for the smaller garden as it seems to have inherited some of the dwarfing characteristics of M. *liliiflora* 'Nigra'. 'Iolanthe' performs very well at Sherwood and I was surprised some years ago to see that her AGM had been rescinded. I even enjoy the massive scented flowers of 'Atlas' and more particularly, our guests' reactions to them on seeing them for the first time. It lacks the elegance of 'Athene' but its huge flowers play perceptual tricks with scale. It looks well growing between mature oaks here.

M. *campbellii* 'Betty Jessel' has made a fine almost candelabra shaped tree which outperforms 'Darjeeling'. M. 'Spectrum' took longer than 'Galaxy' to flower profusely but both are excellent plants. I particularly like our accidental siting of 'Spectrum' next to the pale 'Yellow Fever'. Many of 'the yellows' are proving to be good plants and for us have the advantage of flowering frost free in the coldest areas of the garden. 'Limelight' is very eye-catching just as the buds are opening. Growing 'Elizabeth' adjacent to an early Knap Hill azalea, 'Lapwing' makes a pleasing and colourful link between two of our National Collections.

M. 'Margaret Helen', named after the mother of Vance Hooper is an outstanding newcomer to our collection. It is not unlike, the also excellent, 'Caerhays Surprise' but displays more red tones.

We have lost M. *sieboldii* ssp. *sinensis* to honey fungus, a great shame as it was a magnificent plant with pendulous sweet scented flowers. M. *cylindrica* and its hybrids are all particularly good; I especially like 'Anticipation', pure white and late flowering.

M. *salicifolia* produces a strong lemon scent when the wood is crushed or the bark scratched. One of its hybrids M. x *kewensis* 'Wada's Memory' is a stunning plant especially viewed from afar. M. *dawsoniana* 'Clarke' has been a good find, the flowers first open in a star like form not dissimilar to M. x *loebneri* 'Leonard Messel' only much larger.

On reading recent editions of the *Journal of the Magnolia Society* and our own Yearbook I can see that Sherwood is losing pace with the flood of new and exciting hybrids. We have planted a collection of Ian Baldick's hybrids but it is too early to assess their qualities yet, although *M.* 'Ruth' certainly put on a good display this Spring.

Since the Millennium we have experimented with growing evergreen Asiatic magnolias. The collapse of a large old oak tree and the clearing of a young beech plantation, ruined by squirrels, provided the best place in the garden to try michelias and manglietias, now all magnolias, of course. Out of the frost and, more importantly, protected from the cold north and easterly winds, most of the plants have survived two harsh winters. *Magnolia laevifolia* is the only plant to have flowered significantly and shows great promise.

MAGNOLIA 'MARGARET HELEN' IS AN OUTSTANDING 'NEWCOMER' TO SHERWOOD   VAUGHAN GALLAVAN

PESTS

The aforementioned squirrels may well turn their attention to magnolias. They are inclined to eat magnolia buds, nip the tops of young trees and, as I recently witnessed at Tregrehan, may extensively de-bark michelias. We have even had trouble with them gnawing aluminium labels. Squirrels pose the most major threat to broadleaved forestry and gardens in Britain. A marksman with an air rifle shot 26 of them in the garden last year but more damage has been done this year, most probably by juvenile males arriving from neighbouring territories.

Deer were a problem before a fence was erected in the mid-1990s. This has been very successful in keeping them out. Rabbits have been increasing over the past ten years, before then they were barely present. Young trees are protected within a low chicken wire cage – we found rabbit spirals were inclined to cause the bark of magnolias to soften and rot. The rabbits tend to be a nuisance, spoiling paths and occasionally exposing tree roots

but so far have not caused the ring barking that they are renowned for.

We have suffered some storm damage over the years but as we have been careful to plant in sheltered sites this has not been too bad. I have noticed that *M.* 'Yellow Lantern' seems to be particularly prone to wind damage but recovers quickly as it is so vigorous.

Honey fungus has claimed some magnolias but they do seem to have a greater resistance to it than other genera.

Phytophthora deaths occur in some of the areas where drainage is impaired and mostly seems to claim young plants. Care not to over-water or indeed over-feed with nitrogenous fertilisers is advisable. Mound planting and improving the soil structure with grit and organic matter also help reduce the danger.

ON PROPAGATION

We have been buying seed from the Magnolia Society seed counter, some of it open pollinated and some deliberate crosses made by Dennis Ledvina.

I've found dabbling in hybridization to be fun, though it is still too early for me to see the flowering results yet.

Growing magnolia from seed is easy provided that some basic principles are followed.

Fruits may be collected when ripe, ideally just as the red coated seeds are beginning to show. Seeds are taken from the fruit and soaked for

MAGNOLIA DAWSONIANA 'CLARKE' IS WELL WORTH SEEKING OUT   VAUGHAN GALLAVAN

about 24 hours when the red protective layer will soften and be more easily removed. The seeds should then be placed in damp perlite in sealed polythene bags and placed in a refrigerator over the winter.

I sow seeds in 5 litre pots which provide an ample root run for the first season with about 5 seedlings per pot. It is advisable to cover the pots to prevent seed loss to mice.

Seed raised plants seem to grow very well and quickly establish but may take many years to flower for the first time. This isn't always the case, I believe that *M.* 'Apollo' flowered in just two years from seed.

Plants raised from cuttings have also been quick to establish and have the advantages of being known stock and flowering relatively quickly. Many magnolias may be raised from cuttings, either under polythene or mist where available. Scions from young wood give the best results.

Layering is possibly one of the easiest methods for increasing stock. I prefer large stones to wire pegs for securing low branches to the ground. I have tried air layering with sphagnum moss but find that birds like to take it for nest material – they puncture the polythene and the layers dry out.

It is essential in some cases to propagate by grafting. This seems to be the most common method used by the nursery trade. However, we have lost more plants to graft failure than through any other cause. Sometimes stock and scion look incompatible and untidy looking grafts have appeared to be points of entry for honey fungus My only attempts at making grafts have been by chip budding. For perfect compatibility I have budded scion wood onto seedlings of the same plant. The resulting graft unions are almost imperceptible and although I'm sure this technique would be impractical on a commercial scale I would recommend it for amateur growers.

PLANTING AND AFTER CARE

Magnolia roots develop rapidly and plants may become pot bound and growth checked.

It pays therefore to get the plant into open ground as early as one dares. I make a decision based on whether the plant looks robust and sufficiently developed to survive one week between watering sessions. This usually means that it will be in at least a 3 litre pot and will be a minimum of 50 cm tall.

I prefer spring to autumn planting for magnolias, especially where the young trees are being taken from a protected environment. By late spring the risk of frost has diminished and the ground has warmed enough for the plant to actively grow. By the end of its first season it will have acclimatised and hardened off. Autumn planting may increase the dangers of frost damage both to the bark and also, in the event of prolonged frost, to the roots. It is essential to keep spring planted trees watered through their first two seasons and also to provide some protection from slugs and snails. Application of organic mulch helps to retain moisture and suppress weed growth and those weeds that do establish are more easily removed.

Transplanting is best avoided but can nevertheless be undertaken with care. Magnolia roots are fleshy and easily crushed or snapped. It is never advisable to lift the root ball by the tree's stem, instead, spreading the weight by using sacking or a similar strong fabric underneath helps to reduce the risk of damage. I have had most success with transplanting as the ground is warming and as growth is active. If moving a large specimen is unavoidable it may pay to cut the roots within a 'liftable' circumference with a sharp spade in the season preceding the transplant, giving them a chance to heal and regenerate. We have successfully moved a well-established *M.* x *soulangeana* 'Just Jean' using a mini digger. Growth was checked for the remainder of the season but the tree has grown vigorously since. A reduction in crown by as much as a third is advisable either before or after a major move. Careful attention to regular yet moderate watering after a stressful move is paramount and misting the leaves late in the day also aids recovery.

Those with access to hydraulic digger mounted tree spades should experience successful transplanting.

Ground conditions at Sherwood vary from heavy, poor draining clay, to thin top soils over dry shillet and more favourably, areas of deep loamy drift. I have abandoned deep ground preparation, that seemed to make good sense in the past, in favour of mound planting, especially on heavier ground. I rarely prepare more than one spit deep but do improve conditions over a wider circumference.

When growing in grassland I remove a circle of turves to about a six feet diameter and invert

A TALE OF TWO GRAFTS: *(LEFT)* **A POORLY MATCHED STOCK AND SCION**
(RIGHT) **THE ALMOST IMPERCEPTIBLE UNION BETWEEN SCION WOOD GRAFTED ON TO ITS OWN SEEDLING PROGENY, IN THIS CASE** *M.* **'BETTY JESSEL'**
VAUGHAN GALLAVAN

THE COMBINATION OF *ACER PALMATUM* WITH *MAGNOLIA* 'ATLAS' PERFECTLY DEMONSTRATES THE DECORATIVE VALUE OF AUTUMN COLOUR IN MAGNOLIAS

VAUGHAN GALLAVAN

these in a single layer around the circumference. I apply layers of Cornish grit, leaf-mould, some slow-release balanced fertiliser and well-rotted compost, which these days I work into the underlying soil using a 'Mantis' cultivator. This machine doesn't create the panning associated with flat-tined rotavators.

Most of the magnolias that we have planted have been containerised and may have required a degree of root untangling before going into the ground. Care is taken to not plant too deeply as the lower stems are prone to rot in these circumstances.

I drive stakes in before back filling to avoid the danger of root damage. Staking requirements vary and although it is better to allow the stem to sway, the root ball needs to be static. In the case of particularly leggy or vigorous young trees, full length stakes or long bamboo canes may be necessary for a short period.

For the most part we have aimed on giving each tree the space to grow as a single specimen. Some exceptions to this rule have been with *Magnolia stellata* and some of the De Vos and Kosar hybrids. I think, however, that some of our spacing may seem naive in 30 years or so and some painful decisions may have to be taken.

Pruning is not essential but may be required for shaping, under-planting and sometimes in the aftermath of a storm. Any pruning which requires the removal of large limbs I feel is best undertaken in July or August so that callus wood has a chance to develop and harden off before the first frosts. Some have a tendency to produce vigorous shoots from within the crown which are best removed, albeit for aesthetic reasons.

THE FUTURE

Though a great fan of Plant Heritage and National Plant Collections I have sometimes been distressed by the need to plant a magnolia in any space with adequate room for a tree. This is purely a function of making a collection of trees in a relatively small area and it is fortunate that a wide variety of trees were already in place before the garden achieved National Collection status.

At a mere fifteen acres, the garden has almost reached capacity. We have endeavoured not to overstock, open spaces and vistas being treasured. We have done very little planting since Sir John died in 2009 and further additions to the collection will be as replacements for dead plants or those that have been superseded in quality. There is scope for spilling over into the adjacent meadows and woodland but this is not currently under consideration and, in fact, the future of the collection is uncertain at the moment as Sherwood may be on the market for sale in 2014.

Vaughan Gallavan

is Head Gardener at Sherwood

Magnolias at Wentworth Castle

MICHAEL KLEMPERER

THE ESTATE, HALL and landscape of Wentworth we see today are very much the product of envy, pride and competition, all of which started with a great pioneer in the early eighteenth century.

The estate itself now comprises 660 acres of parkland and some 60 acres of gardens, standing at an elevation of 600ft on the eastern flank of the Pennines, near Barnsley.

The climate is about 2–4°C cooler, and somewhat windier than most places with a magnolia collection in the UK. In addition, because of our situation in the lee of the Pennines, we are in a rain shadow and so have considerably less rainfall than those sites in the west of the country.

The gardens are located on Coal Measures sandstone with a thin, acid sandy soil overlying it, which provides a suitable growing medium for ericaceous plants such as the species of *Rhododendron* and *Magnolia*, and *Camellia* x *williamsii* that make up the three National Collections held at Wentworth today.

In the past the landholding was considerably larger, with gardens of over 90 acres, and more than 2000 acres of parkland; it has its roots in the aristocracy, as opposed to the gentry or squirearchy. Historically, such estates were the largest in the country; the owners typically had holdings of over 20,000 acres and were very often members of the nobility. Their incomes were considerable, with Bateman, in his 1874 survey of the landowners of Britain, putting the annual income of the Earl of Strafford – who held Wentworth at the time – at over 175,000 guineas. This goes some way to explain the grandeur of the stately home and grounds that Wentworth Castle Heritage Trust is in the process of restoring.

MAGNOLIAS AND RHODODENDRONS ASSOCIATE WELL TOGETHER IN THE WILDERNESS GARDEN

PETER CLEGG/WENTWORTH CASTLE

HISTORICAL BACKGROUND

There has been a village at Stainborough – the original name of the Wentworth estate – since Domesday but there is no recorded evidence of a hall on the site at that time. There was, however, an estate (of some sort) recorded in Norman times, with various features,

MAGNOLIA CAMPBELLII

WENTWORTH CASTLE

including a Norman arch of an unknown structure (not necessarily a hall), still remaining in the home farm area.

In the seventeenth century, the Cutler family, owners of Stainborough, as it was still known, had the Hall rebuilt but in 1708 the estate was sold to Thomas Wentworth, 1st Earl of Strafford. His family estate was across the valley to the east, at the village of Wentworth. He bought the property as a challenge to his cousins at Wentworth Woodhouse (some 10 miles to the east) who had inherited the family estates in difficult circumstances. The rival branches of the family hated each other, and vied with each other in landscaping excesses in attempts to outdo the other.

The Earl's early career was spent abroad representing Queen Anne as a special ambassador in Berlin, and there he became influenced by the highly formal continental gardening styles prevalent in Europe at the time. He began laying out his gardens in the new French/Dutch formal style, aided by George London and Henry Wise, the Royal Gardeners and Nurserymen who worked in this style. The landscape and gardens themselves were portrayed by Leonard Knyff in 1714. The depiction shows a series of long avenues stretching into the park and the gardens comprising of a series of formal parterres. In the parkland proper the woodland is dissected by a series of radial avenues, some in a Union Jack shape, reflecting on a massive scale the style of the gardens.

Features of the gardens included the Wilderness – a formal affair of cut/clipped evergreen oaks with an underplanting in a Union Jack form; waterworks including a cascade and large fountain at the front of the house; parterres; a bowling green; avenues; a deer park; woods intersected by radial rides; Queen Anne's obelisk; Lady Lucy's Walk and the gun room/bath house.

A walled kitchen garden, fruit garden and Orangery were built in 1728 at the time of the first head gardener, John Arnold, and the Earl also built a mock medieval castle which gives the site its name.

When the Earl died in 1739, William, the 2nd Earl, created yet more garden and parkland features, and softened the formal landscape to resemble the Brownian (after Lancelot 'Capability' Brown) English landscape style. He created the Palladian Wing of the house in c.1762 with a huge Serpentine lake and various monuments including the Tuscan Temple, Gothic Styled Umbrello, Steeple Lodge, the Sun Monument and the Pillared Tuscan Barn.

The gardens and parkland underwent a series of other developmental phases after this time which included the planting of a tremendous collection of Hardy Hybrid rhododendrons in the Middle Garden, gleaned from various specialist nurseries in the Yorkshire and Nottinghamshire area. It is in this period of the mid-nineteenth century that the collections really started (although the Earls were avid pioneers of planting and acquired stocks of seeds and plants from the Americas in the eighteenth century), and the current legacy of magnolias and rhododendrons really stems from this period.

The gardens were remodelled as the century progressed to include a large and impressive walled garden (over six acres) with attendant staff; the Victorian Flower Garden (a remodelled eighteenth century bowling green); the fernery and, of course, the magnificent Compton and Fawkes Conservatory of the 1880s which is now being restored, thanks to funding from the Heritage Lottery Fund, ERDF, English

Heritage and the Country Houses Foundation. This building, which pioneered electric light, was filled with a range of tender plants including tree ferns, citrus trees, orchids and palms, and provided the ultimate showcase of that particular Earl's horticultural ambition.

In the 1920s the conservatory was remodelled, along with the Azalea Garden, to incorporate a collection of tender camellias and rhododendrons.

The Wentworth Estates were extensive, and included landed properties in Suffolk and Scotland which were sold off as the twentieth century progressed, with Wentworth Castle being sold to Barnsley Corporation as a teacher training college in 1948. The gardens and parkland suffered from neglect as a result, with horticulture being encouraged by the Northern College for just a brief period when it took over from the Corporation in 1978. With help from the Manpower Services Commission some attempts were made to restore the grounds and a fine collection of rhododendrons, magnolias and camellias was built up which formed the basis for the current National Collections.

The Wentworth Castle and Stainborough Park Heritage Trust was formed in 2002 with the purpose of restoring the gardens and park including its monuments and plant collections. To this end, over £20 million of restoration projects have been accomplished on the hall, monuments such as the Rotunda, as well as the wider landscape. The site has been open for just over 5 years and is already attracting over 60,000 visitors annually.

THE NATIONAL COLLECTION OF MAGNOLIAS

The National Collection of Magnolias is planted throughout the Middle Garden(s) and Formal Wilderness. It contains 30 taxa, 17 subspecies and 18 varieties with a further addition of 13 species in the year 2012. Of them all, I am personally drawn to the simplicity of *Magnolia kobus* and the purity of the flowers of *M.* x *soulangeana* 'Rustica Rubra'.

The collection was started in the late 1970s by the Head Gardener, Derek Rogers, now retired, the first introduction being *Magnolia sieboldii* ssp. *sinensis* shortly followed by *M. sieboldii*, *M. wilsonii* and *M. globosa*. The site is exposed in many places and the decision was taken to plant these first accessions on a south

facing slope below the castle monument, sheltered by large trees. In all, 62 specimens were planted. The disadvantage is, of course, that it is dry, and can be shady, so there is a constant demand for water, and regular canopy thinning of the surrounding trees.

Elsewhere in the Formal Wilderness and Middle Garden, the thinning out and cutting back of mature trees and some Hardy Hybrid rhododendrons, as a result of the restoration project, has enabled specimens to be planted, which have shown great promise in the better soils.

In the sheltered beds surrounding the Victorian Flower Garden, specimens of *Magnolia biondii* and *M. rostrata* have been planted to test hardiness in what is the most sheltered part of the site. They join *M.* 'Heaven Scent' and *M. sieboldii*, amongst others, to form a fine backdrop with the Hardy Hybrid rhododendrons in this formal garden.

PROBLEMS WITH NATIONAL COLLECTIONS FOR SMALL SITES

The major problem, with such a large site and limited resources, is labour, and the hierarchy of priorities, rather than the cost of buying specimens. It is possible with small budgets to buy small quantities of stock each year to renew

MAGNOLIA 'STAR WARS'

WENTWORTH CASTLE

THE MAGNIFICENT CONSERVATORY soon to be restored and landscaped with additions to the National Plant Collections

PETER CLEGG/WENTWORTH CASTLE

and improve collections. With the site at Wentworth undergoing (and having undergone) considerable development in the last 5 years, the pressures of weeding and maintaining a large and complex site often eat into the time demands of staff, and this impacts on our ability to manage and label the National Collections. In addition, collections need experienced horticulturalists (with an interest in the plant specimens involved) to run them, which requires longevity of tenure with staff. Wentworth has had many changes over the last few years but fortunately we have been lucky enough to retain staff that do have an interest in maintaining those collections; without that continuity the collections would quickly become compromised.

The practicalities of watering and maintaining a collection in a 60 acre garden have also to be borne in mind, with concentration on good preparation of planting holes being required to give a strong start to new specimens in the thin sandy soils of the site.

It is often unappreciated by those wishing to start National Collections that databases need to be kept and maintained and labelling machines operated (both of which are potentially fiddly and expensive) and these need to be regularly updated by trained personnel. Without considerable input and help from partner organisations the best laid plans can go awry.

THE FUTURE OF NATIONAL COLLECTIONS AT WENTWORTH CASTLE

As the site develops, the National Collections need to be regularly updated and curated to strengthen them. This has the advantage of allowing the visiting public an extra interest factor in the gardens, and, as these new areas develop, it enables the Estates Team to introduce previously unrepresented varieties in those plant collections into the new schemes. With the restoration of the conservatory, over 30 additional specimens are being added to the National Collections, with new planting both internally and along the terracing, and in the wider surroundings of the build.

Wentworth is a charitable trust and we are fortunate enough to have a large and active volunteer force which add to our staff numbers twice a week. Part of our remit (and challenge) is to incorporate those interested volunteers with our trained professionals to facilitate the development of a pool of knowledge to help with the task of maintaining the National Collections. We have already trained certain volunteers to operate the engraving machine and manage the databases, and as the project continues we will add to their numbers.

Another area for the future of our National Collections is to integrate them into our active outreach and education programme as a learning resource; to tell the stories of the plants and those who collected them to a younger audience.

Finally, it is important to remember that in historic landscapes (Wentworth is the only Grade 1 listed landscape in South Yorkshire) we have a duty to preserve the legacy of what went before, and work on forging a garden that future generations can appreciate and enjoy. National Collections make up an important component of that legacy.

Michael Klemperer

is Head Gardener at Wentworth Castle

Beyond the Rubicon: conservation of New Zealand rhododendron hybrids

KATHRYN MILLAR & GORDON BAILEY

RHODODENDRON 'LADY DOROTHY ELLA'

CANTERBURY RHODODENDRON SOCIETY COLLECTION

NEW ZEALAND IS KNOWN AS AOTEAROA by the Maori, a name which means 'Land of the Long White Cloud' and derives from the fact that when approached from the sea, the land appears shrouded in low cloud. With this evocative image in mind, it is easy to picture the whalers and sealers of the southern oceans who had shore bases in New Zealand as early as the 1700s and were fortunate to trade with the Maori who grew sweet potatoes in their vegetable gardens.

European pioneers, pre 1840 – some of them farming squatters from Australia – by necessity put survival of themselves, their family, and animals before flower gardening and it was not until the late 1800s that a few wealthy settlers began establishing gardens such as those their families had on the great estates of the United Kingdom – bringing into New Zealand shrubs and trees of quality, usually in wardian cases, and occasionally as seed.

Rhododendrons are not part of the natural New Zealand flora, the first to arrive being those imported from the United Kingdom ex Hooker's collections.

New Zealand growers of rhododendrons enjoy a wide range of climate because the two main islands extend over a thousand miles in a north-south line with a maximum width of 200 miles, the west coast being wetter than the drought prone east coast. Summer is two months longer than in the United Kingdom,

RHODODENDRON 'COLLEGE PINK'
CANTERBURY RHODODENDRON SOCIETY COLLECTION

circa 1860 by Sir John Cracroft Wilson of Cashmere Estate near Christchurch. In India he had served in what is now called Uttar Pradesh with its many hill stations at altitudes of 6000–7000ft where he collected seed of the Himalayan *Rhododendron arboreum*.

Within the campus of the University of Christchurch is the Ilam garden and home of Edgar Stead from 1917 to 1950. His hybrids from the Cracroft red *R. arboreum*, named for location points in the garden, e.g. 'Ilam Kaka' was near the Kaka's (parrot) cage, are now at risk because they tend to be leggy, and not favoured. Their recorded conservation is in the hands of the Pukeiti Rhododendron Trust and also Heritage Park Trust, home to the original collections of the New Zealand Rhododendron Society.

The Canterbury Rhododendron Association is conducting an important exercise in conservation, assembling a collection which includes almost all New Zealand hybrid registrations and some species selections (Kingdon-Ward to the present day), with careful recording of the original crosses or collection numbers. For Canterbury, I continue to record the pedigree of plants as listed originally, resisting lumping in this respect; and being rewarded by unexpected matchings up with other plants from a seed pod distribution.

The Tannock Glen collections of the Dunedin Rhododendron Group situated on the outskirts of Dunedin City has similar objectives, and the

however out of season frosts following late snow on the Southern Alps can wipe out flower buds on camellias and magnolias, as well as rhododendrons. Many climate zones exist; in Auckland and Tauranga, vireyas may be grown with ease and a proliferation of registered seedlings has resulted. In sheltered micro areas throughout New Zealand may be found pockets where maddenias are grown in profusion – such might be valleys near Dunedin, or the valleys of Banks Peninsula near Christchurch, resulting in a number of registrations of excellent forms of selected species or first cross hybrids.

According to 1850s local legend, the first rhododendrons which came into the port of Lyttelton near Christchurch in the South Island, sat forlornly on the wharf awaiting their owner's arrival by horse and cart from his property in the foothills of the Southern Alps 60 miles distant. These plants, and their open pollinated seed were the parents of many fine hybrids and species seedlings still to be seen in the environs of country estates.

CONSERVATION METHODOLOGY

When making decisions about preservation of historical rhododendrons (for the purpose of these notes, principally the hybrids) the oral history, now for the most part written, was invaluable. An early importation of significance was the packet of seeds brought to New Zealand

RHODODENDRON 'LALIQUE'
CANTERBURY RHODODENDRON SOCIETY COLLECTION

Dunedin Botanic garden has a proud history of plant breeding and selections of quality, currently growing from seed for distribution to collections, plants which may otherwise be lost to cultivation.

A few knowledgeable enthusiasts also maintain and add to their collections of significance as do proactive nurseries dedicated to the preservation and conservation of at risk plants.

Without researching and recording oral history from senior members of the Association over the past decade, we would by now have lost track of the whereabouts of many species and hybrids of significance – however many remain vulnerable. The general membership endeavour to stay vigilant, adopting realistic local conservation procedures. During the 1980s we became aware of how many registered and unregistered superior plants would be lost to recognition as their owners died, and also pressing was to record the whereabouts of named species forms.

In 1998, the publication of *Crossing the Rubicon, a Handbook of New Zealand Raised Hybrids* gave the rhododendron enthusiast information about rhododendrons developed in New Zealand. (An unexpected and ongoing benefit from advising on the preparation of a second edition has been members and growers providing information about where other New Zealand hybrids are located whereupon we usually advise on the steps necessary to propagate such a plant.) Fifteen years after publication the NZRA Trials committee and other discerning folk have realised that within the pages are potentially superb garden plants, and these, as Gordon Bailey notes later in this article, will be assessed for commercial potential.

In discussing preservation and conservation, I note that the hybrids developed at Ilam permeate the early decades of rhododendron hybrids in NZ, not least because so many successful breeders used seed or pollen or grew on open pollinated seedlings sourced from there.

In 1931, when the Rhododendron Association was formed in the United Kingdom, there were four New Zealand members including Mr Stead; he went on to be the Founding (1944) President of the New Zealand Rhododendron Association. During visits to the great UK gardening estates he observed the plants of collectors such as Hooker. Using his importations from the UK, most of them gifts, he was successful in breeding to New Zealand conditions (especially Canterbury with its hot dry and windy summers); registering plants with the RHS in London; and writing for their journals. Edgar Stead was instrumental in conserving bloodlines of precious first crosses; his practice was to load boxes of seedlings to give away into the boot of his car and, through visiting friends for Sunday lunch on country properties often over hundred miles away, he encouraged the

RHODODENDRON 'RUBICON'

GARTH WEDEMIRE

growing and conservation of thousands of seedlings, the best of which can still be seen today. An acknowledged ornithologist, on one occasion he exchanged a bush canary egg for very special seedlings of ex Hooker intro-ductions. Mr Stead registered many fine plants with the RHS and was very particular with selection criteria. The public visiting Ilam during open days are sometimes critical of plants without labels, and astonished when I supply the missing information – that the plants (never named) are from Mr Stead's rigorous selections: usually two for the garden, two or three for distribution to friends or sold and the rest destroyed. Friends always knew if they had the best or second best seedling of a cross.

Time passed and throughout New Zealand the collections and gardens of pioneering enthusiasts became part of city developments or were handed down in families where great care was taken of the plants but nothing known of their breeding or which needed to be taken extra care of. In the period following the Second World War the newly established New Zealand Rhododendron Association (NZRA) (1944) was instrumental in encouraging conservation, although they may not have described it as such, and today we are proud of the success we have had in that field. Thousands of seedlings grown at Massey College (now University) were distributed to members; some fortunately were named and registered.

New Zealand now has stringent bio-security laws, making it close to impossible to introduce new material. All the more reason to search out through the Association's Trial Programme the best of the past and the present, thus providing new material for the rhododendron enthusiast.

THE TRIALS PROGRAMME INITIATIVE

We assess hybrids in a trial programme with the eventual outcome being successful introduction to commerce, and thus conservation. For many years the NZRA and the Pukeiti Rhododendron Trust awarded, on the recommendation of assessors, an Award of Distinction (AD). In recent years the Council placed all award proposals in abeyance, and commenced a trial programme. I invited Gordon Bailey president of the NZRA and also the NZRA Trials Committee to comment.

He writes: 'Since 2005 the NZRA have been undertaking trials of New Zealand bred rhododendrons with the eventual aim of determining whether a plant could be awarded an Award of Distinction.

To be considered for an AD the plant would have to be easily propagated, and perform well across many climate zones in ordinary garden situations.

There are three trial sites reflecting the wide climatic variation experienced across New Zealand. The sites are Heritage Park Trust Garden at Kimbolton, (formerly the NZRA's garden), Pukeiti Rhododendron Garden in New Plymouth and Marshwood Gardens, a private garden owned by Geoff and Adair Genge in Invercargill.

Initially, bud wood was sourced from all manner of rhododendrons that someone thought would be good to trial, without much thought being given to actually whether the plant would do well in general, in a garden situation, could be easily propagated etc. Many were just one-off favourite plants of well-meaning individuals.

As the trials progressed it became obvious that many of the early plants sourced for trial were not going to do well at all and struggled to score points, be it through slowness to flower, poor leaf quality, non-vigorous growth and the like. This brought about a re-think of how to choose future plants for trial.

It was agreed that the trials committee had a good in-depth knowledge of what plants existed across New Zealand that were locally bred and were actually good 'doers' and thus more likely to score favourably in a trial situation. In other words, why not start with something that may actually pass the test rather than something that hasn't a hope.

This is where we are at now. We do have rhododendrons from the earlier trial period that have passed and others are undergoing further evaluation. We run two evaluation score forms, one for hardy rhododendrons and the other for maddenias and vireyas due to the marked difference in growth and flowering habit between the two groups.'

Thus the NZRA has decided to identify plants of excellence, and promote those to a status of commercial popularity and thus safety. You may ask, as do I, what should we do about the hundreds of plants named, many of which are registered. For many years the flower was paramount, often on the show bench; folk waited for years for a nurseryman to supply their order, only to be disappointed when the plant was leggy or disease prone or hated sunshine.

So to sum up, we are looking at conservation of hybrids with the potential to be widely grown garden plants of excellence, and secondly, on an informal basis within the Regional Rhododendron Groups, the

TOP ROW, LEFT TO RIGHT: *RHODODENDRON* 'IVAN WOOD', *R.* 'BARBARA JURY'
MIDDLE ROW, LEFT TO RIGHT: *R.* **'FELICITY FAIR'**, *R.* **'CORAL QUEEN'**
BOTTOM ROW, LEFT TO RIGHT: *R.* **'ORTON BRADLEY'**, *R.* **'ILAM CREAM'**

CANTERBURY RHODODENDRON SOCIETY COLLECTION/JOY O'KEEFE

RHODODENDRON 'IRENE STEAD'

CANTERBURY RHODODENDRON SOCIETY COLLECTION

major collections as noted and through private individuals, we aim to preserve named hybrids.

We simply cannot do as King George VI did when he moved the fabled rhododendrons of Tower Court to the Valley Gardens, although just recently the Canterbury Rhododendron Association gave such a project a good try. They learnt that to place a 'rescued' collection within an existing collection compromised both; the outcome being formulation of a policy that the next time we are asked to relocate a collection in its entirety, we will find new homes for the best plants rather than relocate them all. However, had we not done so, the last remaining plant of *Rhododendron* 'Dame Cecily Pickerill' would have been lost forever.

Preservation of the unique collection of 'made in New Zealand' rhododendron hybrids is important, the 'what to do' of 'conservation' is difficult and even more important.

REFERENCES ■ Millar, K, Coker, M. *Crossing the Rubicon*, Canterbury Rhododendron Association, (1988). (*Beyond the Rubicon* to be published March 2013. Millar, Coker and Hughes.) *NZRA Jubilee Bulletin*, New Zealand Rhododendron Association, (2004). Postan, C. (Ed) *The Rhododendron Story*, p208, RHS, (1996). Stead, E. Rhododendrons in New Zealand, *Rhododendron Year Book*, RHS, (1947). Woodruff, P. *The Men Who Ruled India: The Guardians* (Re. Sir John Cracroft Wilson), Jonathan Cape, (1955). Notes from Viru Viraraghavan, (India).

Kathryn Millar

is a Past President of the New Zealand Rhododendron Association and author of Crossing the Rubicon, a Handbook of New Zealand Raised Hybrids

Gordon Bailey

is immediate Past President of the New Zealand Rhododendron Association

Gardening with camellias for scent

CAROLINE BELL

WE TAKE FOR GRANTED the scent of roses although not all roses are scented; of camellias, the opposite is true: we tend to assume they are not scented, but in fact there are a considerable number which are, depending on the right ambient conditions. The Australian, Stirling Macoboy, in his *Colour Dictionary of Camellias* (Lansdowne Press, 1981), describes how the scent of the pink *Camellia japonica* 'Scented Treasure' (1950), bred by Harvey Short in California, attracted him from 'a distance of many yards'; but the wafting of camellia scent in this country does not seem to happen unless the conditions are exceptional, such as under glass on a very hot day. Usually, we have to come very close, by a matter of a few inches, to the individual flower to smell its sweet scent. Camellia scent varies in intensity and has been likened to apple blossom, roses, hyacinths, carnations and even, in the case of *C. japonica* 'Aroma' (1963, USA), to Easter lilies. But it is beyond the scope of this article to make more than a simple positive assessment of scent.

As Bill Ackerman says in his book *Beyond the Camellia Belt* (Ball, 2007), *'Floral fragrance is a very ephemeral characteristic and its full appreciation is dependent upon both environmental conditions and human perceptions.'* Regarding subjective human perception, he continues *'the sense of smell varies between individuals, ranging from those who lack it (not just older people) to those who are especially sensitive. Also, what may be a pleasant fragrance to some may be neutral or unpleasant to others. This last difference is especially true regarding the fragrance of some blooms of* C. sasanqua, C. oleifera, *and* C. hiemalis. *Here, the quality of the fragrance (or odor) is characterized as being musky or pungent.'*

I have tried to make an objective assessment of scent by using the International Camellia Register, which is now available on-line, as my primary source for confirming my impression of scent; and failing that, I have checked that a camellia is considered scented or fragrant by two camellia specialists. I shall be using the words 'scent' and 'fragrance' hereunder inter-changeably, and trying to follow the breeder's or the Register's terminology: even in the Register the words are not used consistently as the entries are composed by different people and are not standardised. I find that I instinctively designate 'scent' as a stronger word, and I use it in preference to 'fragrance' altogether, but many authors use it the opposite way, so the reader must please have patience.

As so many people consider the autumn flowering camellias to have a 'musky odour', which is not always sweet, I am omitting this group from consideration. I shall describe scented *Camellia japonica* cultivars, including the Wabisukes and Fishtails, as well as Higos, a few *C. reticulata* crosses, *C. saluenensis*, including the *C. x williamsii* hybrids, inter-specific hybrids with *C. fraterna*, *C. transnokoensis* and *C. lutchuensis* parentage, and finally the new Chinese species.

CAMELLIA JAPONICA 'HIKARUGENJI', an old Japanese cultivar whose scent is reliably inherited by its offspring   SALLY HAYWARD

CAMELLIA JAPONICA 'MARIANN'

CHRISTOPHER BELL

At the end of the article the reader will find two tables detailing another 125 scented camellias which I have not encountered but which are said to be scented, either by the Register, which is the majority, or, in the case of a further few, confirmed by two secondary authorities. But first, I shall consider the prerequisite conditions likely to enable camellias to scent successfully.

PREREQUISITE CONDITIONS

My enthusiasm for camellias started with scented varieties, in what I imagine are the almost perfect environmental conditions of the Isabella Plantation in Richmond Park, London, where there is high dappled shade from established woodland which helps moisture retention and creates good conditions for scent when temperature, humidity and air movement are right. We do not all have these ideal conditions, indeed in my Devon garden I do not, as it is on the side of a valley at 450 feet above sea level. It is mostly open and sunny and can be windy at times, but even without ideal conditions I find it is worthwhile growing camellias for scent. The right atmospheric and climatic conditions as well as the 'right' time of day, which is obviously when the day is warmer,

seem to make a considerable difference as to whether any plant, including a camellia, performs up to its scented best, as warmth releases the volatile oils which make up scent. The late Kenneth Hallstone, a Californian camellia breeder for scent, researched the emergence of scent. In his article 'Fragrant Camellias' (in Macoboy) he observes how temperatures above 60°F or 15°C, together with some moisture, enhance and strengthen the scent. Regarding moisture, he describes how the scent from a bloom can improve after a night wrapped in moist materials before going out to the warmth of the show bench. I have observed this to be true every so often at camellia shows; for example, at the recent RHS Rosemoor Show, I smelt some scent which would almost certainly have been lacking outside, on the loose pink peony form *C. japonica* 'Tiffany' (1962, USA) which is a parent of 'Scentuous' and originally from Japanese seed collected by Ralph Peer. The need for some moisture is not only an issue for camellias: I have observed it even affects the scenting of roses, the reliability of whose scent we rather take for granted.

Helga Urban, German author of the slim pamphlet, *Fascination, Scented Camellias* (Ulmer, Germany, 2009. Available in translation as an E-book by Klaus Urban, Ulmer, 2010.) describes the research into the *'exact origin of this subtle (camellia) scent'* by the Japanese firm Shisheido, whom I see from their website have specialised in cosmetics since 1872, even adopting the camellia as their logo as long ago as 1916. By dissecting *'petal by petal, a perfumer found that the source of the scent was at the base of the stamen filaments, ovary, and the pistil, and a floral nectar was being secreted abundantly to form dews on the petals.'* This crucial research demonstrates the importance of the stamens. Helga Urban's solution to problems with cold and scent is to grow camellias in pots and bring them out in April when the weather near Frankfurt warms up. She adds that most *C. lutchuensis* hybrids are conveniently late flowering. I do not have the facility for this practice, so my experience is entirely from growing camellias outside. Our winter temperatures are inconsistent and usually milder, so that I can enjoy *C. japonica*

'Shiro-wabisuke' outdoors on a mild January day. Urban believes 10°C is the lowest temperature at which 'the essential oils' which create the scent, can release it. I confess to not having done any scientific measurement of temperature against sampling of scent yet, having read her book in May, at the end of the season; but I believe her 10°C (50°F) minimum is broadly accurate.

The final prerequisite for scent is probably the presence of stamens in the flowers as it is from their bases that the volatile oils which make up the scent are released. However, I have found one case where scent does occur without any stamens, where there are just petaloids. This is on the red *C. japonica* 'Mariann' (1984, Garner, USA) which is an anemone form with petaloids in my garden and despite having no obvious visible stamens, there is good reliable scent in the depth of its flower head. 'Mariann' has a poor growth habit as well as being slow growing, but its flowers are a joy to smell. I feel that it may be something of an anomaly, but perhaps some of the anemone form hybrid camellias listed in *Table B*, which I have not encountered, also only have petaloids.

This imperative for scented camellias to have stamens has been underlined for me by growing camellias which have been bred abroad for scent, but which do not live up to their billing in my garden. Indeed, most recent breeding for scent has taken place in the warmer parts of New Zealand, Australia or the United States, and I find that some of these plants do not perform here. As they seem to change to a flower form without stamens, I am led to conclude that the lack of stamens or reduced stamens affects their ability to produce scent. So, if a camellia is described as a formal double then it has absolutely no stamens and, probably emphatically, no scent. (There may be one exception: *C. japonica* 'Fragrant Girl' included in *Table A*, which I have tried to check without success, as there are no references to it other than the Register. I think the description could be a mistake as it should surely be anemone form, as it says it has petaloids.) Other camellias have consistently single or semi-double flowers and so always have stamens; these stamens could be producing scent to attract pollinators, although this by no means predicates scent.

Otherwise the flowers are either formed like a peony (or informal double), a rose or an anemone, with either stamens and/or petaloids intermingled.

I have found cases of changing flower forms for all the doubles in camellia literature and as is well known, camellias can exhibit different flower forms at the same time on the same plant, and flower forms can vary from year to year as influenced by the weather and indeed climate. The form a camellia takes in the southern hemisphere can differ markedly from how it performs in the northern hemisphere, for example, inter alia, 'Emmett Barnes' (1949, USA) is said in Jennifer Trehane's book *Camellias, The Gardener's Encyclopaedia* (Timber Press, 2007) to be a semi-double in cooler climates and a loose peony form elsewhere, and 'Alice Cutter' (1974, USA) is said in Macoboy's book to be semi-double originally, but a larger anemone form 'in cooler climates and moist areas'. 'Joan Trehane' (1979) is a vastly improved formal double or rose form here, but, as Jennifer Trehane says, was an insignificant 'coarser' peony form plant in its New Zealand home.

The underlying issue is that many *Camellia japonica* cultivars are inherently unstable not only in the colouring of their flowers as we know well, but also in their flower forms. Since *C. japonica* varieties are used so widely

CAMELLIA JAPONICA 'EMMETT BARNES'
is floriferous and reliably scented

CHRISTOPHER BELL

in breeding with the other species, including *C. lutchuensis*, and some hybrids have three-quarter *C. japonica* parentage, then this can affect many camellias. Tom Savige, first compiler of the International Camellia Register, remarks in a chapter of Macoboy's book how 'Camellia japonica *and its hybrids are particularly noted for their sporting propensity and many hundreds of horticultural varieties have been obtained by propagating these.'* He explains that this happens because the present garden forms of the species have been subject to so much breeding over the centuries *'of endless inter-crossing and out-crossing'* so they *'have accumulated a very high genetic variance.'* He describes various lines of sporting camellia 'descent'. One of these, it is interesting to note, is a scented 'sports family' which he traces from the scented 'grandparent' *C. japonica* 'Hikarugenji', (1859, Japan) (also well known by its synonyms 'Herme', 'Souvenir de Henri Guichard' and 'Jordan's Pride'). Eight out of the eight sports or descendants from this cultivar are known to have scent in some conditions: 'Beni Botan' (1877), 'The Mikado' (1900), 'Beauty of Holland' (1938), 'Colonial Lady' (syn. 'Fragrant Striped') (1938), 'Look Away' (1938), 'Orchid Pink' (1939), 'Quaintance' (1951) and 'Spring Sonnet' (1952), all originating in the USA. None of these camellias are known to me except 'Spring Sonnet', which, as far as I know, is not known for scent here. Yet it is amongst the few recommended for scent by Nuccio's Nursery in California.

Interestingly enough, I found that 'Spring Sonnet' did have a faint scent this year when smelt growing under open glass on a hot March day at Marwood Hill Gardens in North Devon but the flower did not look like the strongly stamened semi-double form to be seen on the American Camellia Society website, instead being an informal double. As a sport of 'Hikarugenji' maybe this is not surprising, as it is notoriously unstable. Jim Stephen's wonderful website www.jimscamellias.co.uk displays a photograph of 'Spring Sonnet' which is a beautiful, informal double bi-colour of white and pink with deeper pink margins, with the possibility of a few hidden stamens underneath in the centre: this is how he has seen and photographed the plant growing outside in the National Collection at Mount Edgcumbe and indeed, this is just one of several other examples of the variability of its form to be seen on-line. I use the example of 'Spring Sonnet' to demonstrate a camellia whose flower form changes, thereby, I believe, affecting its ability to scent.

It is not, I think, the presence of sun, or lack of it, or the level of light intensity which provokes the change: rather it is the degree of warmth from the sun and the overall warmer temperature. It is cooler growing conditions which cause problems for camellias, known to be reliably scented abroad, when their stamens are lost or reduced.

From these general observations on the prerequisites for scenting in camellias, I shall now describe the camellias themselves.

A SCENTED, WILD COLLECTED *CAMELLIA JAPONICA* at Stone Lane Gardens in Devon
PAUL BARTLETT

CAMELLIA JAPONICA CULTIVARS

The *C. japonica* cultivars we see in gardens have highly refined characteristics which suited the prevalent fashion of their era of breeding. Plants raised from wild collected material should display the original attributes of the species, and when I came across wild collected *C. japonica* in May, at Stone Lane Gardens in Devon, I was not at all surprised to find a plant with scented flowers among a group of small red singles. The seed for these specimens was collected by Kenneth Ashburner in 1980 from Ullung Do island, 75 miles north off the coast of Korea in the Sea of Japan. The scented one had a very small dark red flower of about 3cm diameter with dark glossy leaves, forming a well-shaped dense bush growing in open woodland amongst the very beautiful *Betula* and *Alnus* National Collections. I have recently learnt of 'Tokai' (1975, Japan) which is a deep red single, starting off campanulate and then opening wide, originating from Izu Ohshima Island, Japan where many wild collected camellias have origin-

CAMELLIA 'SCENTED SUN', a reliable floriferous cultivar with good scent   CHRISTOPHER BELL

ated, and 'slightly fragrant' according to the Register; its name follows that of a pre-1700 camellia which had been lost from cultivation, but is now, presumably, restored. The Register records that 'Kaori-gozen' (meaning Fragrant Lady) (1990, Japan) was wild collected from the inhospitable volcanic island of Miyakejima, some 112 miles south of Tokyo, and is a pale pink, striped light red, cupped single. These three examples from the wild confirm that scent is a trait possible in the genetic inheritance of *Camellia japonica*.

I will return to the many other Japanese contributions to scent, but first I shall consider cultivated varieties of *C. japonica*, in colour groupings for ease of reference.

The classic white single camellia, 'Alba Simplex' (syn. 'Snow Goose'), first recorded in 1816 (England, Rollinson), was my first scented camellia. A good specimen grows in the Isabella Plantation but I have found it difficult to obtain, so instead I have started to grow its close relative the floriferous 'Charlotte de Rothschild' (1964, England) which may be a better single white. I recently encountered 'Henry Turnbull' (1950, Australia) another sweet smelling single white growing at Marwood, an International Camellia Garden of Excellence. My favourite white, however, is 'Emmett Barnes' (1949, registered USA, originating from seed sent from the Tokayama Nursery in Japan) which is semi-double in cool

climates like ours in the UK. My plant has a slightly weeping style which was frustrating at the outset; it flowers prolifically with glossy dark leaves to set it off, and exudes a reliable sweet scent when smelt close up, unless it is very cold.

Another impressive semi-double white is 'Scented Sun' (1985, USA) bred by Kenneth Hallstone, which has complex parentage but mainly *C. japonica*, thematically fitting in best here, and flowering late in the season with good scent. It has large flowers, sometimes with a faint pink mark and is vigorous in growth and very satisfactory in all respects. Its lineage includes 'Mrs Bertha A. Harms' (1948, USA) which is reputedly scented and has been much used in breeding. Marwood grow it in their greenhouse under the recognised synonym 'Mrs Bertha A. Harms Blush', and on a hot day recently, I found there was a slight scent which might come through better in the USA, where it is registered as a semi-double, rather than the rose form I saw.

There are three bi-colours of note: 'Jack Jones Scented' (1985) is a floriferous blush to light pink with pink stripes which also grows in the greenhouse at Marwood. I grow it but so far it has not been scented: I have heard of it scenting elsewhere, whereas in my garden it is an informal double without stamens as yet. It is registered as a semi-double chance seedling arising at Marwood but propagated by Jack

Jones in Georgia. 'Nuccio's Jewel' (1978, USA) which we all know and love, as it has such beautiful flowers of white shading to orchid pink, has had considerable consistent scent this year for me against a west facing wall; its growth is dense and slow, but it makes up for it with such a flower. Finally, there is 'Carter's Sunburst' (1959, USA) which I grow and notice can demonstrate complete variety within its double flower form even on the same day; it is a very pale pink, striped dark pink, said to have scent but never seems to, probably because it has lost its stamens. However, just after a warm spell this year, I noticed there were a few stamens on one of the blooms and when brought into the warmth of the house there was a definite hint of scent.

Macoboy rates two others for scent in the blush to pink semi-double group which I do not grow: 'Erin Farmer' (1956, USA) and 'Cara Mia' (1960, USA). There is also *C*. x *vernalis* 'Star above Star' (1964, McCaskill, USA), well known for its occasional January flowering, appearing as a beautiful semi-double blush with darker lavender toning on the American Camellia Society website, whereas in my garden it becomes an informal to formal double without stamens and no scent so far. I have smelt its scent most years at Marwood, where it is grown outside, sheltered against a high wall under

AN UNKNOWN RED SCENTED *C. JAPONICA*
with finely serrated acuminate leaves
CHRISTOPHER BELL

TREWIDDEN'S C. 'SCENTED RED', growing in Devon
CHRISTOPHER BELL

high dappled shade, usually having a hose-in-hose semi-double form. Growing unreliably scented camellias against a wall would seem to be a good idea.

There are a number of scented red single *Camellia japonica* varieties. I grow 'Scented Red' (1987), first recorded by Trewidden Gardens in Cornwall. I grow another reliably scented single red which is 7cm across but which regrettably had no name on purchase; it was slow to establish, but now flowers prolifically and has glossy long leaves. I am trying to identify it and my latest guess is that it is 'Paul's Jupiter' (1904, UK) but this is unproven. I have not come across 'Odoratissima' (1866, Australia), so I cannot confirm its reputation for scent, but it is usually considered to be a rose-red, large semi-double, blooming late. 'Jimmy Smart' (2005, Devon) is another single with many stamens, whose parents are 'My Darling' (1947, USA) said to be scented, and 'Clarise Carleton' (1956, USA); it was bred at Marwood by the late Dr Smart and the original (now large) plant is definitely scented, but on its progeny recently I could not detect any scent, for which I have no ready explanation beyond the vagaries of our weather.

As for red doubles, I have mentioned 'Mariann' already with enthusiasm. I have recently detected a light scent in the well-known 'Guilio Nuccio' (1955, USA), a superb, large coral-red semi-double. It is a seedling of the red semi-double fishtail 'Mermaid' (1947, USA) which is well known in the USA, and said to be scented, but distinguishable from 'Kingyo-tsubaki' (*see later*), which is a single camellia. In view of its parentage, it is not surprising 'Guilio Nuccio' sometimes has a light scent. 'Kramer's Supreme' (1957, USA) which is a large red, full peony form is well known to be scented under glass or in a hot climate. More reliable, and with a light scent sometimes outside, is 'Aaron's Ruby' (1956, Louisiana, USA) which is a vigorous upright cultivar able to cope with shade and flowering very well for me; it is a bright, metallic red peony to anemone form but with some stamens, unlike 'Mariann'; its habit is preferable to 'Mariann', but its scent is not as strong. There is also the light red peony 'Jim Finlay's Fragrant' (1995, New Zealand) ('Nioi-fubuki' x 'Kramer's Supreme'), which has been specifically bred for fragrance, but seems not to be available in this country yet – a photograph can be found in Jennifer Trehane's *Camellias, The Gardener's Encyclopaedia*.

Turning to the true pinks, there is the well-known 'Scentsation' bred by Nuccio in California (1968) which I have yet to find true to its name after purchase. In the greenhouse recently at Marwood I could smell its scent on a warm day, and there were some visible stamens on those flowers, as there are in the excellent photograph in Jennifer Trehane's book. In my garden, 'Scentsation' stays as a formal to informal double with maybe a few hidden stamens especially as the season progresses, but it is unscented, upright and vigorous. I have tried it in several different positions, from sunny, semi-shaded to full shade, where it is currently, but with no improvement. I have now purchased a third plant from a different vendor in an attempt to find a truly scented clone and if I can keep the stamens visible on 'number three' on next year's flowers, perhaps I will have a scented plant at last. But if, as I suspect, it has less to do with the right clone and more to do with

the right weather and garden conditions producing enough stamens, then I am unlikely to succeed. Macoboy acclaims David Feather's 'Temple Incense' (1967, USA), a large pink semi-double, for scent, and noted as such in the Register; in English conditions, at Marwood some years ago, it was noted as being well scented in their outside collection. I have already mentioned the pink 'Scented Treasure' (1950) which performed so well for Macoboy in Australia.

There is also a group of light pink Japanese singles which are scented. First, 'Suibijin' (1934–5, Japan), which is its prior name in the Register, but grown under its synonym 'Yoibijin' by Spinners in Hampshire, with a large plant to be seen there. It has an attractive flesh-pink cupped flower and Spinners say it flowers from October to April. David Trehane in the Wisley handbook on camellias (RHS, 1980) uses the name 'Yoibijin' as a synonym

PRETTY C. 'SUIBIJIN' (SYN. 'YOIBIJIN') *growing at Spinners in Hampshire*

ANDY ROBERTS, SPINNERS NURSERY

for 'Taro-an' (1933, Japan) which he describes as having pendent branches and pale pink single flowers; various authors describe the cupped flowers of 'Taro-an', famously used in the Tea Ceremony, and all agree it is scented and historic. It seems likely that this breeding strain comes from a scented wild *Camellia japonica*. The larger flowered 'Akebono' (1931, Japan, although it is sometimes called 'Shin-akebono' after being renamed in the USA) is more of a peachy pink, flowering from as early as January; I believe this may be the same as 'Ake-no-shin', a good specimen of which grows at RHS Rosemoor, flowering early and it seems to be a good performer.

WABISUKES & FISHTAILS

The Japanese prefer single camellias and have concentrated their breeding work on singles over many centuries. The Wabisuke group of single trumpet shaped *C. japonica* varieties, first mentioned in 1695, have been given species status in the past in Japan. Their origin has long been discussed: most recently a morphological and cytological study by Takayuki Tanaka of Tokai University, Japan presented in the ICS Journal 2012, posits the view that all plants in the Group descend from 'Tarokaja' (1739, Japan) which he says is

CAMELLIA '**SHOWA-WABISUKE**'   ANNE BERLIN

an F1 hybrid between *C. pitardii*, imported from China, and wild *C. japonica*, originating in Japan, possibly as early as 1549. He notes their distinctive broadly elliptic and finely serrulate leaves with cork warts. The descendants of 'Tarokaja', considered to be Wabisukes in Japan, are botanically distinct because they are infertile with an abortive androecium and ovary. Although they are still being catalogued and bred in Japan, where they are popular for the Tea ceremony, there are probably only four in this country. First, 'Shiro-wabisuke' (1844, Japan) which can be seen in the Isabella Plantation as well

as at RHS Rosemoor, and starts to flower usefully in early January. I am fond of its small single white campanulate flowers and it stands up to the weather, then dropping its spent flowers almost too quickly. It is a most desirable camellia in many respects, flowering prolifically, although its faults are that it is slow growing and its scent can be elusive in very cold weather. 'Tarokaja' (syn. 'Uraku') which I find is a much less useful shrub as it tends to be leggy as well as very slow growing, is pink. It is grown well at Greencombe, near Porlock, by Joan Loraine, and also at Rosemoor. Research shows that a camellia called 'Magali' (1937, Belgium) may be the same plant but grown under a different name in France and Belgium. The white flushed pink 'Showa-wabisuke' (1938) (syn. 'Hatsukari' in Japan) which some consider to be the same as the 'Apple Blossom', mentioned later, is floriferous and makes a good shaped camellia quite quickly with more open flowers which are delightfully scented. There is also the Fishtail cross 'Kingyoba-shiro-wabisuke' (1989, Japan) which has so-called fishtail leaves as the leaves resemble the tail of a goldfish; this has a larger single white flower which is 'wide-campanulate', but has the characteristic sweet Wabisuke scent.

Researching this article, I see there are 82 Wabisukes listed in the Camellia Register, all originating from Japan, while Tanaka takes only 19 to study; he includes 'Kon-wabisuke' (1937, Japan), mentioned by Macoboy and on the French website www.lovcam.org where it is said to grow at Trevarez in Brittany. It has dark red, small tubular flowers and the Register records it to be very similar to 'Kuro-wabisuke' (1960, Japan) with the same dark red flower with dark stamens and is available in Australia. There is also 'Beni-wabisuke' (syn. 'Kosho-wabisuke') (1844, Japan), a small 'dull red single', included more as a botanical curiosity, with a photograph in Jennifer Trehane's book, but neither she nor the Register mentions scent for them. Nuccio's Nursery website, under the heading of 'Fragrance Camellias', lists additionally the Japanese 'Fukurin-wabisuke' (1971) as a small, light pink bordered white single, and 'Hina-wabisuke' (1968) as a small rose-pink single.

C. 'KINGYO-TSUBAKI', an old Japanese cultivar with interesting fishtail leaves   PAM HAYWARD

The Register reveals that there are 31 Fishtail Camellias which are all varieties of *C. japonica* with the name 'kingyo' or 'kingyoba' included, which translates as goldfish leaved; the Fishtail group definitely has two more members in this country: 'Kingyo-tsubaki' (1789, Japan) (syn. 'Quercifolia'), a good specimen of which can be found at Abbotsbury Subtropical Gardens in Dorset, where its weeping graceful style is evident; it has rose-red, scented single flowers peeping out from under the leaves and a good central boss of stamens. Second, a cross of this with *C. saluenensis* made in 1935 at Kew and named after its originator 'C. F. Coates' (1948) where the flowers are similarly single but rose-pink and smaller; neither flower prolifically. There is also a scented fishtail camellia growing at Knightshayes Court, a National Trust garden near Tiverton, Devon, which came from the National Trust garden at Greenway in Devon under the name 'Quercifolia'; it is a single of light crimson fading to rose-red. Greenway, once owned by relatives of the Williams family of Caerhays, have also given three slightly different pink to rose-red fishtails to Hill House Nursery in Devon, so there may be seedlings around in old gardens: the Register comments that it does set seed.

The Register lists several variegated Fishtails and when names such as 'Kaori-shibori-kingyoba' (1988, Tokyo) are translated as 'Perfumed Variegated Fishtail', it is clear there are other scented ones too. Whether there are further garden worthy plants for us is another matter.

HIGOS

Mention must be made of the Higos, originating from the old Higo province now the Kumamoto prefecture in Kyushu, Japan, and being simply a specific style of *Camellia japonica* flower which is single with 100 to 250 stamens according to Dr Franco Ghirardi, who is the leading Western expert on them. Both Jennifer Trehane in *Camellias: A Gardener's Guide to the Genus* (Batsford, 1998) and Jutta Fischer in *Success with Camellias* (Munich, 1989, with an English version, Merehurst, 1994) believe them to have, as the latter puts it, 'a delicate scent'; Jennifer Trehane recommends 'Okan' (1982, Japan) and 'Nioi-fubuki' (1971, Japan) itself registered as fragrant. I have now been able to test the scent of the latter at Marwood and it was, indeed, strongly scented. Few Higos are available in Britain, but it is interesting to see that when their Japanese names are translated some of

C. 'OKAN' is a beautiful, lightly scented Higo cultivar   MICHAEL SHUTTLEWORTH

C. 'NIOI-FUBUKI', an attractive strongly scented Higo cultivar   MICHAEL SHUTTLEWORTH

them indicate scent, as in 'Nioi-fubuki', meaning 'Scented Snow Storm', and with any others having 'Nioi' in their name also being scented, such as 'Nioibeni' (1978) (Perfumed Red), or 'Nioi-fukurin' (1983) (Perfumed Border). 'Akatsuki-no-kaori' (1964) (Fragrance at Dawn) and 'Tenko' (1965) (Heavenly Fragrance) are also listed as fragrant by the Register. I have recently purchased 'Higo-kyo-nishiki' (1912, Japan) which is white, striped and splashed crimson, and I consider it to have a slight scent.

Jim Finlay of New Zealand used 'Nioi-fubuki' in his breeding programme for scent to create several new scented camellias. I have produced *Table A* to cover other *C. japonica* varieties which are either registered as fragrant or scented, or confirmed as such in two secondary sources, and it includes several of his.

CAMELLIA RETICULATA & C. OLEIFERA CROSSES

I encountered the *Camellia reticulata* hybrid 'Interval' (1972–3, USA) bred by David Feathers (a notable breeder for scent) in the ideal conditions of sheltered woodland just yards from the sea at Abbotsbury Subtropical Gardens in Dorset. I found it had a light scent to its large flat pink semi-double flowers with plenty of stamens, but no details of its parentage appear

in the Register. Crosses between *C. reticulata* and *C. sasanqua* produced the 'Girls' group bred by Howard Asper: these are 'Show Girl' (1965, USA) which I grow, 'Flower Girl' (1966, USA) and 'Dream Girl' (1966, USA). I find these can occasionally have a slight musky fragrance, but as they flower from early in January, the colder weather usually extinguishes it. 'Dream Girl' was crossed with the species *C. oleifera* to give 'Sugar Dream' (1984, New Zealand) which is registered as fragrant and has anemone form pink flowers with a cream boss of petaloids; my plant has not settled down to flower yet, so I cannot comment.

C. oleifera has been used for breeding programmes because it is both lightly scented and particularly hardy, taking more than – 15°C in its hardiest form, 'Plain Jane' (2002, USA). It flowers from November to February, which is useful. I grow it, but I find it does not flower every year, and is difficult to site: it needs the right ratio of part sun to shade. Ideally it would probably like a wall to ensure regular flowers, but it is now too big. When it flowers, and over the nearly 20 years I have grown it, it has done so satisfactorily perhaps five times, it has white, single, mildly scented flowers, sometimes cupped with a hint of pink, the scent reminiscent of the muskiness of *C. sasanqua*. It is narrow and upright, and then spreading.

C. RETICULATA HYBRID 'INTERVAL' flowering at Abbotsbury in Dorset   SALLY HAYWARD

CAMELLIA SALUENENSIS & THE C. X WILLIAMSII HYBRIDS

There are several tree-like specimens of the species *C. saluenensis*, with light pink single flowers, in Antony Woodland Garden, Cornwall, another ICS Camellia Garden of Excellence; I have found a mild scent on some of them. Better still for scent is *C. saluenensis* 'Apple Blossom' which I acquired from Trehanes under that name. Its origin is not completely certain: it is said by Jennifer Trehane to have been introduced by Nuccio's Nursery in 1955 and to have some *C. japonica* blood with the *C. saluenensis*; Nuccio's themselves only list the 'Showa-wabisuke' mentioned earlier, and as 'Apple Blossom' flowers early it would suggest it may have some Wabisuke blood; indeed it looks very like 'Showa-wabisuke'. It is a single, white toned pale pink, and consistently and reliably, delightfully scented, hardy to at least −12°C without damage in my garden. It is not surprising, therefore, to find that some of the *C. x williamsii* camellias who all trace their parentage back to *C. saluenensis*, should have some scent.

'Mary Jobson' (1962) bred at Caerhays by JC Williams, has always been known to have some scent; it is a single in a classic 'Cornish pink' colour, though of an awkward pendulous habit until established. I have found it to have reliable scent. Another pink I want to rediscover is 'Parkside', which appeared in our Yearbook in 1959 and originates from Windsor Great Park; it is a single to semi-double and a good specimen is to be found in the Isabella Plantation. 'Bow Bells' (1954, Marchant, UK) is a bell-shaped pink semi-double described as scented in the Register, as is 'Parkside'. I grow 'Free Style' (1980, USA) bred by David Feathers, named to indicate its varied flower form; its usually peony flowers are prolific in the classic pink and this year it has even produced some semi-double blooms. It was always said to be scented and lives up to its reputation consistently. Its fault is that it is slow-growing. 'Senorita' (1975, Les Jury, New Zealand) which I have just started to grow, seems to have a lovely sweet scent; it is a wavy, informal peony double of the classic pink and as its parentage is *C. saluenensis* and the already mentioned 'Hikarugenji', perhaps

C. 'FREE STYLE', a lovely *C. x williamsii* with good scent   CHRISTOPHER BELL

scent should not be such a surprise. The pink single 'Mary Larcom' (1962, Caerhays) is said to be 'sometimes fragrant' by Jennifer Trehane amongst others.

Outside the classic pinks, there is 'Hooker' (1973) which I smelt at Tregrehan several years ago and which was bred there by Gillian Carlyon, ('Paul's Jupiter' x 'Salutation'); bringing *C. japonica*, *C. reticulata* and *C. saluenensis* into the mix, it has an unusual large coral pink single flower which is semi-cupped. Finally, there is Nuccio's 'Freedom Bell' (1965, USA), of unknown parentage which is an upright, red semi-double with an interesting triangular bell shape to the flowers; it is well named as it flowers prolifically, and I find it a very satisfactory camellia to grow after the first few years of slow growth.

INTER-SPECIFIC HYBRIDS

The introduction of the miniature flowered scented species of *Camellia lutchuensis*, *C. transnokoensis* and *C. fraterna* from Japan and China to the USA and Australasia from the 1950s has led to extensive hybridisation, to take advantage of the scent of the former two in particular. The most favoured species is *C. lutchuensis* as it is said to have the strongest scent of all, described by some as sweet like honey. All three have hardiness which is borderline to doubtful. As the years have gone by, the simple inter-specific hybrids have developed to second and third generation crosses. I have given a synopsis of some breeding details where possible; my observation is that the trend that seems to be developing is for three-quarter scented *C. japonica* parentage. *Camellia japonica* seems to remain the essential element in breeding new camellias, I presume because of its growth habit, hardiness and its own contribution to scent. Some of the earliest hybrids were what are termed 'cluster-flowering' with miniature flowers; many are slow growing, so suit small spaces, especially if there are walls for shelter.

CAMELLIA TRANSNOKOENSIS   SALLY HAYWARD

Once I have considered the species themselves, I shall look at a representative selection of the breeders, working in turn; I have produced *Table B* to cover more extensive examples of recent breeding of scented hybrids which I have not encountered, but which are registered as scented.

I do not grow any of the straight species as yet, but I am told that both *C. lutchuensis* and *C. transnokoensis* can be grown outside with care in the south and can scent successfully. Jennifer Trehane describes *C. fraterna* as 'not reliably frost hardy'. In their favour is that all three of these species have considerable resistance to petal blight which destroys the beauty of blooms by its ugly brown blotches, so this is a useful additional trait for hybridisers.

Examples of *C. fraterna* crosses have not come my way, but I see that 'Fragrant Fairies' (1994, Australia) is registered as 'scented'; the upright, vigorous, pale pink single with an occasional stripe is a cross with the unscented *C. pitardii* and bred by Marjorie Baker. She also produced the 'fragrant' 'Marjorie's Dream' (1993, Australia) which is a weeping, miniature white peony form and also a *C. pitardii* hybrid. 'Yoimachi' (1982) bred by Dr Clifford Parks of North Carolina (*fraterna* x 'Narumigata'), has been sold by Trehanes for a number of years; it is a white marked pink miniature single, which is said to have some fragrance. These three are

by way of a sample only and I have no experience of growing them.

Of those with *C. transnokoensis* parentage, I am trying the floriferous 'Sweet Jane' (1992, Australia), a seedling of 'Edith Linton' x *transnokoensis* bred by Ray Garnett, which is not registered as scented; it has a very pretty miniature flower of two-toned white-blush to pink, but it stays as a formal double with a few petaloids in my garden, which can be typical of it. Jennifer Trehane's second book describes it as scented. Its leaves have coped with full sun and its blooms have stood up very well to rain and cold. 'Transpink' (2004, New Zealand) a miniature soft pink single bred by Neville Haydon, is a chance seedling of *C. transnokoensis*, said to have an 'appealing honey scent' in the Register and attractive upright growth. Its single blooms could make its scent more reliable here.

The leaves of *C. lutchuensis* and *C. transnokoensis*, and some of their simple hybrids are small, similar to *C. sasanqua*, and their new growth has an attractive pink to copper tone, but I find the *C. lutchuensis* hybrids can scorch or yellow in full sun, so that they have to be carefully sited in semi-shade with shelter from wind; they seem to flower just as well there, which is not what I expected from their labels on purchase. Researching for this article I see *C. lutchuensis* is a woodland plant, like so many other camellia species, native to what were once called the Lutchu or Liu Kiu Islands, now known as the Ryukyu Islands, situated between Taiwan and Japan. Although the two hard winters of 2009 and 2010, where we experienced ten to twelve inches of snow which lingered for several weeks, did not kill my *C. lutchuensis* hybrids, my plants were severely mauled: I lost a large number of leaves with some die back. I would estimate they endured between –9°C and –12°C degrees in sheltered conditions. Even so, I spent some time freeing them from the snow, thereby avoiding further damage to their delicate branches from the weight.

C. lutchuensis hybrids mostly seem to be blush-pink in colour, and the outstanding and most reliable cultivar I grow, and the one which seems to receive the most plaudits generally, is the single flowered miniature 'Quintessence' (1985, Lesnie, New Zealand) ('Fendig's Seedling No 12' x *lutchuensis*); this has a consistent sweet scent making a small, slow-growing prostrate mound which can be used to weep over a wall. It came through untouched in 2009 and 2010, perhaps partly because of its sheltered position; but 'Fragrant Pink' (1966, Ackerman, Maryland, USA) suffered considerably as did 'Spring Mist' (1983, Longley & Parks, USA), but less so, probably because of its more sheltered position, as I grow it on and over a wall. Where 'Spring Mist' hung over the wall, its leaves and stems were undamaged; its faintly scented blooms

are most often a blush formal double, but I see they are registered as semi-double. 'Fragrant Pink' only just survived, losing virtually all its foliage. It has been very slow to flower and its one pink peony form flower a few years ago was not scented. Perhaps in its new (third) position, it will do better. It seems to me that the real cause of these last two camellias remaining unscented in my garden is that they lose their stamens whereas photographs of them growing abroad show them as full of stamens. As 'Fragrant Pink' is sterile, Ackerman then produced the fertile 'Fragrant Pink Improved' (1978) which was 'improved' by colchicine treatment. The Register gives the description of scent as a 'pleasant fragrance similar to sweet osmanthus' and the breeding is *C. japonica* var. *rusticana* Yoshida x *C. lutchuensis*.

I have found very little scent generally in the Ackerman hybrids which I grow. His 'Cinnamon Cindy' (1974) ('Kenyotai' x *lutchuensis*) is also a disappointment as it is meant to smell of cinnamon, but I find it scentless, staying as a formal double, having none of the petaloids which are mentioned in the Register; it has attractive cream to blush-pink flowers, comes out in March and flowers prolifically in nearly full sun. I initially grew it against a wall in full sun, but it outgrew its position and seems pretty robust. I have heard of it smelling in woodland conditions in Devon; it is narrow and upright in growth. However Ackerman's 'Fire 'n' Ice' (1992) (*japonica* x *oleifera*), flowering late in the season, had a slight scent this year, in a new position on a hot day. It has lovely deep red anemone to rose flowers and the slight scent came from the 'ice' of its few but usually visible cream filaments and stamens. It makes a rounded, neat and dense bush quite quickly and the flower form is variable from the semi-double it appears to be in the States. I have read that Ness Botanic Gardens has been trialling many Ackerman hybrids over several years although more for hardiness than scent, as they are reliably hardy further north.

STRONGLY SCENTED *C. LUTCHUENSIS* HYBRID 'QUINTESSENCE', growing outside in Devon   CAROLINE BELL

JIM FINLAY'S *C. LUTCHUENSIS* HYBRID 'SCENTUOUS'

JIM STEPHENS

Robert Cutter, working in California, notably produced two three-quarter *C. japonica* crosses using 'Mrs Bertha A. Harms', namely the red 'Virginia W. Cutter' (1973) and the pink 'Alice K. Cutter' (1974). I have smelt the former in the greenhouse at Marwood on a hot day and it had a slight scent but certainly not the '*C. lutchuensis* fragrance' claimed from US conditions in the Register.

The New Zealand breeder, Jim Finlay has made a special quest for scent to a superlative degree, stating in the 1997 ICS Journal that *'since 1984 I have raised 685 camellia plants in which I have controlled the crosses in my efforts to obtain further fragrant varieties.'* His work started in 1970 and continued until his recent death. Amongst his many, and indeed his first registration is the well-known 'Scentuous' (1981) ('Tiffany' x *lutchuensis*). I find it has a faint fragrance occasionally as a peony flower, but more typically is closer to a formal double, and I have given it more sun with shelter; photographs taken abroad show it has blush miniature semi-double flowers. I have recently started to grow his 'Superscent' (1988) whose ancestry includes 'Mrs Bertha A. Harms', 'Salab' (1971, USA) and 'Spring Sonnet' but no *C. lutchuensis* blood. I grow it in full sun at the moment which may not suit its *C. japonica* style leaves; on my small plant, the scent was good on one flower which was a peony form, and non-existent on its fellow bloom out at the same time

which was a formal double! But its blush to white blooms are beautiful. His 'High Fragrance' (1985) is starting to become available; it has similar parentage and colouring, but some *C. lutchuensis* blood and is said to be a peony form with petaloids and some stamens, and particularly good scent. It sounds promising, and the French growers, Stervinou, commend it on their website for scent saying it is hardy down to –14°C. Our 2010 Yearbook, page 121, recommends the clear pink 'Souza's Pavlova' (1988, New Zealand) given as a peony form in the Register, but which is a semi-double in Sally Hayward's photograph, which bodes well. Its breeding is 'Nioi-fubuki' x 'Scentuous', so it is only one-quarter *C. lutchuensis*. It sounds worth trying. Other Finlay bred camellias may reach us eventually such as 'Hyperscent', 'Scintillating Fragrance' or 'Yummy Fragrance', and others included in *Table B*. Some of his also feature in the *C. japonica* varieties listed in *Table A*. He has used so many combinations of all the camellia plant sources available to him to create new scented camellias, but interestingly he seems to have ended up with more than half *C. japonica* blood in many cases, and regularly used the *C. saluenensis* blood to be found in 'Salab'. ('Salab' is of complex parentage including *C. sasanqua* 'Apple Blossom' and *C. saluenensis* and has, according to the Register, a propensity to set seed readily, which trait has been useful to hybridisers in breeding, but its own fragrance is only described as 'somewhat musky'.) Sadly, I cannot find any information about the reasoning behind Finlay's breeding programme, which might give us more understanding about gardening with camellias for scent.

Jutta Fischer acclaims 'Duftglockchen' (translated as 'Scented Bell') (1990, Germany) (*lutchuensis* x 'Bokuhan'). It was named (but not raised) by her husband, Peter Fischer, of the famous Fischer Camellia Nursery at Wingst in Northern Germany, where there is another Camellia Garden of Excellence; it is cascading and pendulous with salmon-rose single flowers and yellow stamens, like 'Quintessence', but much pinker. From the same cross made by Domoto comes the semi-double 'Scented Gem' (1983, USA) but it is a darker pink miniature with a centre of distinctive white petaloids looking like Iced Gem biscuits. I have no experience of either of these. The pink peony form 'Sweet Emily Kate' (1987, Australia) bred by Garnett is slow growing; it has three-quarter *C. japonica* parentage with one-quarter *C. lutchuensis*, and is commended by several authors including on Stervinou's website, where it is said to tolerate –12°C and be cascading and prostrate, which sounds like the growth habit of 'Quintessence'. I would place more reliability on 'Quintessence' for scent because its flower form is single.

There have been others whose scent seems to be floral but with a different slant such as Ackerman's rose-red 'Ack-Scent Spice' (1981), (*lutchuensis* x 'Fragrant Star'), registered with a 'lemony to spicy fragrance' or 'Hallstone Spicy' (2008) a pink peony form of unspecified parentage with a 'spicy fragrance'. *Table B* contains more descriptions from the Register of the extraordinary and diverse scents of other hybrids.

Japanese breeders are also working hard, sometimes using the Wabisuke Group as their preferred parent with *C. lutchuensis*, and nearly always producing simple single flowers. I wonder

C. 'MINATO-NO-AKEBONO', a Japanese-bred *C. lutchuensis* hybrid with miniature flowers and strong scent   JIM STEPHENS

if these may suit our climate better. 'Minato-no-haru' (1987, Japan) (*lutchuensis* x 'Kon-wabisuke') has peach-pink, fragrant, campanulate small flowers; it is pendulous and floriferous. 'Minato-no-akebono' (1989, Japan) is a seedling of *C. lutchuensis* with a *C. japonica*, from Masaomi Murata, with a very small, pale pink single scented flower with mauve overcast fading to white in the centre. 'Koto-no-kaori', (1990) ('Tokai' x *lutchuensis*) with small rose-red flowers, was named in 1977 in Japan. These three have the special commendation of being listed as 'Fragrance Camellias' by Nuccio's Nursery.

'Takao-no-kaori' (2010, Japan) ('Kon-wabisuke' x *lutchuensis*), which was crossed by Shuho Kirino around 1960, has a profuse, miniature single white flower with red at the petal tips. As mentioned earlier, the word 'kaori' means scented in Japanese, so take seriously any camellia having this in its name. 'Shunpu' (1986, Japan) (*saluenensis* x *lutchuensis*) is a faint-pink cup-shaped single with 'rather strong fragrance' according to the Register. Finally, Dr Kaoru Hagiya of Niigata University who wrote of his hybridizing work in 'Studies in Inter-specific Hybridization of Japan' (*Bulletin of the Seibu Maizuru Botanical Institute*, Vol. 2, 1986), bred the peachy-pink semi-double *C. lutchuensis* seedling, 'Otohime' (Younger Princess) (1986, Japan) from a *C.* x *vernalis* parent; it has flowers in the leaf axils. 'Sotorihime' (Princess in Ancient Japan) (1986) is his light peach-pink semi-double pendent cross of *C. lutchuensis* with a Higo, also bearing flowers in the leaf axils, and there are other 'Princesses' he bred. I look forward to all these Japanese-bred camellias becoming available here.

NEW CHINESE SPECIES

As China has become accessible over the last few decades, further species have been introduced and become available to us. Their year of discovery and place of origin is in brackets, not their registration details. I grow *Camellia grijsii* (1861, China) which is not fully hardy and has white, miniature single flowers scented of aniseed or liquorice; it flowers from early Spring scenting better as the weather warms up. It also has a double form, similarly miniature, which is reputedly even better for scent, named 'Zhenzhu Cha' (1990, China). *C. forrestii* (1912, China) is said to be scented and is being trialled in Britain from Ness

Botanic Gardens (and more extensively since the Group has had access to seed offered in the annual Seed List); it has small white flowers and Jennifer Trehane believes it can take down to –8°C with shelter. I have grown *C. tsaii* (1938, China/Vietnam) which has long willowy leaves and supposedly some scent, but lost it in a winter before 2009, so consider it completely tender. It has been used in hybridization with *C. fraterna* by Betty Durrant in New Zealand to create the slightly fragrant and tender 'Ariel's Song' (1990) which has awkward pendulous branches and single miniature white flowers. I lost my plant in the winter of 2009.

Other species said to be fragrant and not already mentioned are *Camellia dubia, C. euphlebia, C. furfuracea, C. gracilipes, C. handelii, C. henryana, C. kissi, C. melliana, C. miyagii, C. nemotodea, C. nitidissima* var. *nitidissima, C. salicifolia, C. synaptica, C. yuhsienensis,* and *C. yunnanensis.* Some of these seem to be available in the United States, where their scent is commented on, for example *C. yuhsienensis* and *C. synaptica. Camellia sinensis,* the tea plant, is also said to have some scent. Most recently *C. rosthorniana* and its best

CAMELLIA GRIJSII, the species with an unusual liquorice scent   SALLY HAYWARD

form 'Tianshanfen' (China 2012), a small pink miniature single, has been discovered. Some hybridization has started: *C. synaptica* 'Magnolia Moon' (2009, USA) can be viewed on the internet; the Register reveals it to be 'very fragrant' with large white flowers, but says it is unlikely to be that species, and is more likely to be a form of *C. yunnanensis* (1919, China) distributed in the USA as *C. synaptica.*

Dr Hagiya chose to make crosses of *Camellia yuhsienensis* (1965, China) with *C. hiemalis,* of which 'Yume' (1992-3, Japan) (*yuhsienensis* x 'Shishigashira') is perhaps the most well-known and interesting; it is an attractive, small bi-colour single of white with purple-pink shading in the centre, probably flowering from October to March in the Carolinas, and featuring in several continental botanical collections. Finlay's 'Good Fragrance' (2001, New Zealand) ('Fragrant One' x *yuhsienensis*) is a semi-double which the Register says has 'honeysuckle or raspberry scent' and has colouring of interesting shades of pink to orange red. His 'Fragrant Burgundy' (2002), also a *C. yuhsienensis* hybrid, is in *Table B.*

Bill Ackerman used *Camellia kissi* (1820, SE Asia) crossed with a *C. japonica* to produce the pale pink miniature single seedling 'Fragrance of Sleeve' (1984, USA), said to have 'strong' fragrance in the Register. 'Zuiho' (1987, Japan) raised by Ogawa Takeo, said to be fragrant and cold hardy with profuse blooming in the Register, is a white shaded pink cupped single and another straight cross with *C. japonica. C. kissi* is described by Urban as smelling of violets which is appealing. Jim Finlay crossed some of his new scented hybrids onto the recently discovered species *C. chekiangoleosa* (1965) from southern China, producing four scented progeny in 2002, but I have not been able to discover their names, perhaps because they have not been registered. Dr Hagiya also made a cross with the scented *C. japonica* 'Odaira-kaori' to produce the 'mildly scented' *C. chekiangoleosa* hybrid 'Kofugyoka' (1994, Japan) which is a large rose form double red, and 'Seiko-no-yuyake' (1994, Japan) using *C. japonica* 'Tokai' as a parent to yield 'mild' fragrance from a vermilion, cup-shaped single flower.

CONCLUSIONS

Sadly, I have to conclude that some of the new inter-specific hybrids need ideal conditions to be reliably scented outside in the UK. Perhaps the Japanese-bred ones will do better with their single flowers, such as 'Minato-no-akebono' or 'Takao-no-kaori', because of the tendency of some double flower forms to lose some or all of their stamens and thereby their scent. The growth style and hardiness of *Camellia japonica* seems to be an essential element in improving the tender species and it is its

THE FASCINATING FLOWER OF *C. YUHSIENENSIS* HYBRID 'YUME'

STERVINOU CAMELLIAS

scented forms which have appeared in breeding programmes. We should not, therefore, discount the *Camellia japonica* cultivars in our enthusiasm for the more recent hybrids with *C. lutchuensis* although there is no question that the scent from *C. lutchuensis* is desirable and strong when it appears, as for example in 'Quintessence'.

I believe walls are useful for adding to the reliability of scent; my example of this is the case of 'Nuccio's Jewel' in my garden and 'Star above Star' when grown at Marwood. This is something that is well recognised for autumn flowering *Camellia sasanqua* varieties because it is said that the wall intensifies the sun's warmth, thereby helping to initiate flower buds which might not otherwise form; but perhaps this heat also helps the production of scent, by encouraging flower forms with stamens, and once there are stamens, the intensified heat enables the release of the oils which produce the scent. This would make sense of the problems I have experienced with 'Scentsation', whereby it can be found scenting truly when purchased at a nursery where there is a stone wall around it or a polytunnel to cover it; but, when leaving its cosy home to come to our cold draughty gardens, it loses its scent. If some camellias hold on to their scent better because of a wall, that feature would be more important

to them than the high overhead shade that appears to enhance scent in the Isabella Plantation or at Abbotsbury. Similar conditions are to be found in some areas of the National Collection at Antony. At the end of the day, it is all about experimenting with a camellia's position in the garden to find the best spot, which can be a long drawn out process! It is interesting to note that posts on Garden Forum websites from the mild climate of Northern California's Bay area or North Carolina in Zone 7/8 mention problems with camellia scent on, for example, 'Cinnamon Cindy', so this is not only a problem for our climate.

Although it is worthwhile growing camellias for their scent, it is not always an easy task to site some of them to optimise their potential. My top recommendations for reliability would be 'Emmett Barnes', 'Free Style', 'Scented Sun', 'Mary Jobson', 'Shiro-wabisuke', 'Tarokaja', 'Scented Red' and 'Mariann'; but if you have a sheltered warm wall the best choice of all would be 'Quintessence' or 'Apple Blossom' as neither are fully hardy. 'Superscent' might scent reliably, but I have not had it long enough to judge. 'Nioi-fubuki' and 'Kingyoba-shiro-wabisuke' would be good selections from the Higo or Fishtail category respectively. When more of the new Chinese species and Finlay bred camellias are introduced, we may find others which are reliable. I hope you will agree that there are many camellias to try!

Finally, let it be said that outside our world of camellia enthusiasts, it is encouraging to see camellias recognised for scent by Stephen Lacey in his book *Scent in your Garden* (Frances Lincoln, 1991) the major work in this field; he lists 'Scentsation', 'Mary Jobson' and 'Fragrant Pink', but looks forward to more camellias emerging with *Camellia lutchuensis* parentage.

Kenneth Hallstone, in Macoboy, states *'It is surprising to me that more of the camellias do not emit floral fragrance because the seeds have been cultivated for centuries so that their delicate oil could be used in the blending of perfume.'* The Japanese obviously have no doubt as to the significance and worth of the camellia's scent: additionally using scented camellia oil in cosmetics and for hair oil. Indeed, the Western perfume trade has now seized on this and recognised camellia scent by producing 'Eau de Fleur de Camelia' which comes from a Parisian Fashion House, owned, significantly, by a Japanese-born designer, Kenzo; it was launched in Autumn 2011. Others are following suit in the perfume and cosmetics trade with both the scent and oil and a new fashion seems to be developing.

So, the future beckons to scented camellias, and *Deo gratias agimus pro gloria naturae.*

Caroline Bell

has a passionate interest in camellias and has been growing them for 25 years

Table A – Fragrant/Scented *Camellia japonica* varieties

Fragrant japonica	Colour/Comment	Form	Date/Origin
Amy Maryott*	Pink; seedling of Berenice Boddy	Semi-double	1999 USA
Aroma*	Lavender rose; scent of 'Easter lily'	Semi-double	1963 USA
Athena*	White marked deep rose	Anemone	1958 USA
Barbara Mary*	Blush pink; from Waterhouse	Peony	1965 Australia
Bessie Dickson*	White	Anemone	1982 USA
Billie McCaskill	Pink; chance seedling	Semi-double	1955 USA
Blood of China	Red; buds not hardy	Semi-double	1938 USA
Breath of Spring	Pink; from David Feathers	Semi-double	1953 USA
Brodie's Pink*	Pink; occasional red stripe	Single	1947 Australia
Buddy*	Pink; purple cast	Semi-double	1964 USA
Candy Stripe* (Waterhouse)	White striped flecked red; from Waterhouse	Single	1965 Australia
Carol Lynn	Large white striped red	Semi-double	1957/8 USA
Cucamonga*	Red/vermilion sport of Kramer's Supreme	Rose double	1981 USA
Esther Moad	Pink; seedling of Akebono	Peony/semi-double	1943 USA
Fragrance*	Light rose	Peony	1954 USA
Fragrant*	Red	Peony	1958 USA
Fragrant Boutonniere*	Bright red; from Finlay	Peony	1992 NZ
Fragrant Frill*	White-pink	Peony/semi-double	1962 USA
Fragrant Girl*	Shell pink; chance seedling	Formal double? with petaloids in centre	1992 USA
Fragrant Jonquil*	White	Anemone	1953 USA
Fragrant Star*	White	Semi-double	1958 USA
Grand Slam	Large red; from Nuccio	Semi-double	1962 USA

Fragrant japonica	Colour/Comment	Form	Date/Origin
Grantham's Fragrant*	White	Semi-double	1961 USA
Heaven Scent*	Rose red	Peony	1951 USA
Heavenly Fragrance*	Pale pink	Peony	1958 USA
Iced Fragrance*	White	Semi-double/peony	1990 Australia
Jim Finlay's Fragrant*	Light red; from Finlay	Peony	1995 NZ
Kofu* (Scented Gemstone)	Red striped white; from Funakoshi	Single, cupped	1987 Japan
Kokuryu (syn. Black Dragon)	Dark red	Semi-double	1859 Japan
Koshi*	Purple red; from Izu Ohshima Island	Single, campanulate	1960 Japan
Kramer's Beauty*	Red	Peony	1981 USA
Kramer's Delight*	Pink	Peony	1981 USA
Lazetta*	Red; seedling of Hikuragenji	Anemone	1951 USA
Marie Sivet*	Soft satin pink, from Claude Thoby	Single	1993 France
Nioi-fukurin*	Pink edged white; sport of Nioi-fubuki, Higo	Single	1983 Japan
Parksii* (see image page 148)	Cerise irregular white blotched; imported	Peony	1830 China
Pete's Fragrant Pink*	Pink	Semi-double	1995 USA
Pink Poppy*	Pink, Higo style	Single/Semi-double	1938 USA
Prime Fragrance*	Red; from Finlay	Peony	1995 NZ
Pristine Fragrance*	Red; from Finlay, Higo blood	Peony	1994 NZ
Scentasia*	Red; from Finlay, Higo blood	Peony	1997 NZ
Scented Fireglow*	Orange red; from Finlay, Higo blood	Semi-double	1995 NZ
Scentimental*	Large red; from Finlay	Peony	1997 NZ
Serenade*	White; seedling of Finlandia	Semi-double	1957 USA
Simeon	Rose red, seedling of Hikuragenji	Semi-double	1950 USA
Smellie Nellie*	White striped red	Peony	1979 USA
Sweet Bonair*	White	Semi-double	1951 USA
Sweet Delight*	Rose pink	Semi-double/peony	1947 USA
Sweet Sue*	Currant red	Peony	1956 USA
Taffeta Tutu*	Large apricot pink	Semi-double/peony	1960 USA
Tahiti	Red; from EG Waterhouse	Single	1965 Australia
Tama-ikari*	Pink; seedling of Nioi-fubuki	Single	1971 Japan
Vega*	Pink; from Claude Thoby	Peony	1993 France
Vernice Anne*	Pink	Peony	1975 USA
Violet Bouquet	Violet, chance seedling	Anemone	1970 USA
Wheeler's Fragrant*	Large white-pink; seedling of Hikuragenji	Semi-double/double	1949 USA
Yixiang* (Released Fragrance)	Pink	Peony/rose	1990 China

* = Described as Scented or Fragrant in the International Camellia Register

Table B – Fragrant/Scented *Camellia* hybrids

Hybrid Name	Colour/Breeding	Form/Style/Scent comment from Camellia Register	Date/Origin
Adrianne Ila*	Light pink; *pitardii* x *fraterna*	Single, miniature; weeping, slow	1995 Australia
Aromatica*	Variegated pink; from Finlay	Large semi-double/peony	2002 NZ
Ack-Scent*	Shell pink; from Ackerman	Peony; 'deep spicy fragrance'	1979 USA
Ack-Scent Pink*	Rose; from Ackerman, seedling	Rose; 'strong sweet fragrance'	1981 USA
Ack-Scent Sno*	White; from Ackerman, seedling	Semi-double/anemone; 'sweet fragrance'	1981 USA
Ack-Scent Star*	White; from Ackerman	Anemone/Rose; 'sweet fragrance'	1981 USA
Allure*	Pink variegated white	Semi-double/peony	2006 US
Asatsuyu*	Soft pink with graduation; *rusticana* x hybrid Tiny Princess; from Dr Hagiya	Small semi-double	1983–4 Japan
Autumn Fragrance*	Light pink; from Finlay	Single	2002 NZ
Bridal Fragrance*	Large white; from Finlay	Peony	1996 NZ
Cinnamon Scentsation*	Pink & white; from Ackerman	Single; sport of Cinnamon Cindy; 'highly fragrant'	1995 USA
Dame Silvia*	Scarlet pink; *japonica* hybrid; from Finlay	Semi-double/anemone; 'floral, rose-like scent'	2002 NZ
Debo*	Red; *japonica* x *vernalis*	Single	1998 USA
Drifting Scent*	Pink; x *williamsii*; from Finlay	Large peony	1994 NZ
Escential*	Pink; x *williamsii* x *lutchuensis*; from Lesnie	Small single; 'scented'	1993 NZ
Esme Spence*	Pink blush; *japonica* x *fraterna*	Anemone	1977 NZ
Fairy Blush*	Soft pink; from Jury; *lutchuensis* seedling	Miniature single	1994 NZ
Feather's Darling*	Red; *reticulata* Buddha x (*fraterna* x Salab); from Feather	Large semi-double	1984 USA
Fimbriated Fragrance*	Red; *japonica* hybrid; from Finlay	Rose; fimbriated petals; 'light scent'	1999 NZ
Fragrantasia	Bright pink; from Finlay	Single; 'strong fragrance'	2002 NZ
Fragrant Burgundy*	Dark rose red; (Mrs Bertha A Harms x Salab) x *yuhsienensis*; from Finlay	Peony; 'strong, attractive rose + clove scent'	2002 NZ
Fragrant Cascade*	Pale pink; from Finlay	Single; weeping habit; *lutchuensis* scent	1994 NZ
Fragrant Drift*	Pink; some *lutchuensis*; from Finlay	Peony; slow growth	1994 NZ
Fragrant Genesis*	Light red; *japonica* hybrid, with no *lutchuensis*; from Finlay	Anemone; 'honeycomb fragrance'	1999 NZ
Fragrant Jewel*	Pink; *japonica* hybrid; from Finlay	Anemone/peony; 'carnation + clove scent'	2002 NZ
Fragrant Joy*	Lavender pink; some *lutchuensis*; from Ackerman	Rose miniature; 'highly fragrant'	1983 USA
Fragrant Lady*	Ivory pink flushed; from Finlay	Large semi-double; 'light fragrance'	1997 NZ
Fragrant Legend*	Bright red; *japonica* hybrid	Peony	2002 NZ
Fragrant One*	Pink; *japonica* hybrid; from Finlay	Large single; 'light fragrance'	1998 NZ
Fragrant Pathfinder*	Deep pink; from Finlay	Large single; 'hay-like scent'	1999 NZ
Fragrant Pixies*	Pale pink; from Mrs Baker; chance hybrid seedling	Miniature single; slow growing; weeping; 'pleasant perfume'	1995 Australia
Fragrant Ripple*	White/pink ripples; *japonica* hybrid	Anemone; 'light gardenia scent'	1999 NZ
Fragrant Ruby*	Red; from Finlay	Large peony; self-grooming	2005 NZ

Hybrid Name	Colour/Breeding	Form/Style/Scent comment from Camellia Register	Date/Origin
Grand Fragrance*	Deep pink; from Finlay	Semi-double	1999 NZ
High Fragrance*	Ivory pink; *japonica* seedling x (Salab x Scentuous); from Finlay	Peony; 'strong *lutchuensis* fragrance'	1986 NZ
Hyperscent*	Bright scarlet; from Finlay	Rose	1994 NZ
I am Fragrant*	Pinks + shading; from Finlay	Large anemone, 'light fragrance'	2002 NZ
Ice Melted*	Light pink; from Finlay	Semi-double	1992 NZ
Intoscent*	Pink shades; from Finlay	Peony, 'moderately strongly scented'	2002 NZ
Julie's Own*	Light pink; flowers profusely along stems	Miniature semi-double, cluster flowers	1993 Australia
Kaori-hime*	Peach red; Wabisuke x *lutchuensis*; from Dr Hagiya	Miniature trumpet-shaped single	1990 Japan
Kaori-ichigo*	Pale pink; *japonica* Bokuhan x *lutchuensis*; from Yoshikawa	Miniature single; dwarf, weeping	1990 Japan
Kaori-nigo*	Pale pink; *japonica* x *lutchuensis*; from Yoshikawa	Miniature semi-double, dwarf	1998 Japan
Kohi*	Pink-crimson; seedling of Hishikaraito x *lutchuensis*; from Mrs Nagao	Very small to small semi-double	1990 Japan
Marna*	Bright pink	Semi-double	1984 USA
Mandy*	Pale pink; *rosiflora* seedling; from Edgar Sebire	Miniature semi-double; weeping habit	1984 Australia
Masterscent*	Coral red; *lutchuensis* hybrid; from Finlay	Peony; 'good fragrance'	1994 NZ
Nanpu*	White-pink; from Dr Hagiya	Small single; Higo-like	1989 Japan
Nymph*	Blush; from O' Toole	Miniature semi-double	1982 NZ
Perfumed Pearl*	Pink; *japonica* hybrid, from Finlay	Anemone; 'light honeycomb scent'	1999 NZ
Paddy's Perfumed*	Pink; from Finlay; seedling	Anemone	1992 NZ
Petite Boucalaise*	Rose; *fraterna* x *japonica*	Small, bell shaped	1993 France
Pink Crepe*	Pink; *pitardii* hybrid; from Baker	Single clusters; slow, weeping habit	1994 Australia
Pink Posy*	Pink; *fraterna* x *japonica*	Semi-double; cluster flowering	1995 Australia
Radiating Fragrance*	Light pink; from Finlay	Rose double; 'fruity scent'	2002 NZ
Salut*	Pink; *saluenensis* x *lutchuensis*; from Mrs Stone	Miniature single	1981 USA
Scented Swirl*	Deep pink; from Finlay; hybrid seedling	Large peony	1994 NZ
Scintillating Fragrance*	Dark pink; *japonica* hybrid; from Finlay	Rose/peony; 'good, full, honey & rose' fragrance	2002 NZ
Softly Fragrant*	Pale pink; from Finlay	Peony; 'light, somewhat spicy scent'	2002 NZ
Spring Wind*	White-pink; *japonica* x *lutchuensis*	Miniature single; 'very sweet'	1984 USA
Sugar 'n' Spice*	Light pink; *saluenensis* x *lutchuensis*, from Lesnie	Semi-double	1993 NZ
Sweet Deborah Jane*	Pink with lighter tones; from Finlay; *japonica* hybrid	Large rose/peony	2002 NZ
Sweet Emma*	Flushed white; from Finlay; hybrid from *C. japonica*	Anemone; 'spicy fragrance'	1997 NZ
Togetherness*	Pink; fraterna hybrid; from Baker	Single, slow growing	1995 Australia
Top Fragrance*	Deep pink; *japonica* hybrid; from Finlay	Anemone/peony; 'light scent'	1999 NZ
Vernal Breeze ('CF44')	White; from Dr Clifford Parks	Miniature single	1994 USA
Yummy Fragrance*	Bright red; x *williamsii*; from Finlay	Peony	1995 NZ
Yoshihime*	Red shades; *fraterna* x *sasanqua* x *japonica*; from Dr Hagiya	Semi-double; leaves silver-green, 'strongly fragrant'	1986 Japan

* = Described as Scented or Fragrant in the International Camellia Register

Rhododendrons to ridicule?

TONY SCHILLING VMH

RHODODENDRON
'CETAWAYO' –
THE EPITOME OF
MELANCHOLY
GLOOM!

SALLY HAYWARD

MANY RHODODENDRONS are of such obvious beauty that only a philistine would have the impudence to criticise them. Even those which exhibit less pronounced virtues, such as the demure *Rhododendron cowanianum, R. nipponicum* and *R. semibarbatum*, should not be denigrated for their understated charm and can safely be left for the connoisseur to cultivate.

No, the rhododendrons I wish to ridicule are those which disappoint and those that simply do not live up to their name or deserve the reputation they have somehow obtained.

This is obviously dangerous ground as one man's meat is another man's poison and fashions come and fashions go. Additionally, I don't believe it is fair to include plants which have a reputation for being invasive. Here we come inevitably to the much maligned *Rhododendron ponticum* which (courtesy of Dr James Cullen) we must now refer to as *R. x superponticum* as the entire band of 'hooligans'

that have taken over vast areas of countryside are recognised as being a bunch of mongrels. If one really wants the true species one will have to obtain it from the wild, or talk nicely to someone at a Botanical Garden.

Peter Cox refers to this plant's tainted reputation as 'ponticum prejudice'. Yes, it is at times annoyingly invasive and is extremely prone to *Phytophthora ramorum* but nevertheless, I and others remain faithful to its merits for it would be all too easy to forget its invaluable involvement in the early story of hybridisation. Harder to take to our hearts are the *Rhododendron ponticum* clones 'Variegatum' and 'Cheiranthifolium'. Worst of all is 'Aucubifolium' which assails one with its yellow spotted leaves.

Inevitably, while considering this topic of 'who likes what' I cast around for various opinions and, perhaps understandably, received some amusing and unexpected answers.

John Gallagher, renowned and respected for his enthusiasm for magnolias and camellias, came quickly to the point by stating (perhaps with tongue in cheek) that he disliked the entire genus!

I next asked the multi-talented Head Gardener of Crarae Gardens, Nigel Price, for his point of view and he surprised me by damning 'all the purples', not just a ponticum prejudice but a far wider ranging colour prejudice which may tempt one to refer the matter to the Race Relations Board! On cross examination he did, however, modify his opinion a little by listing various exceptions. Others I have met with over the years have also flinched from the colour purple, muttering phrases such as 'morgue-like', 'gloomy' and 'darkly depressing'.

One of the darkest purple hybrids yet raised is R. 'Cetawayo', fine if you like that sort of thing, but almost excessively dark flowered and prone to weather damage. Here, it is virtually impossible to pass on without quoting the late James Russell's classic

RHODODENDRON 'JANET WARD' – ALTOGETHER TOO MUCH   SALLY HAYWARD

description – *'a large bush which has all the melancholy dignity of a superb prune mousse.'*

Personally, I generally enthuse over deep coloured rhododendrons, but one I simply cannot warm to is R. 'Praecox'. It must be accepted by many as a welcome and colourful sight in late winter/early spring (its only attribute in my opinion!) but its violet-purple flowers shout too loudly for my liking. I once expressed my opinion to one of my staff at Wakehurst Place and later in the day he came across to me and stated that, following my remarks, he was much inclined to agree, adding that 'it was not so much a colour as more of a noise'!

The list of purples is a long one and does not exclude species. Perhaps the most common complaints come from those who are introduced to *Rhododendron niveum* for the first time as the colour is so unusual. For my part I enjoy its eccentric tinge but I cannot say the same for R. 'Colonel Rogers' (syn. 'Trevarrick') which has been described by some as being 'like a washed out niveum'. Its other parent is *R. falconeri* but it has not gained anything from that; quite the reverse in fact.

Our editor, Pam Hayward, told me that her bête noire is R. 'Janet Ward' which I understand originated as a sport of R. 'Cynthia'. Her reasons for ridicule are due to it looking *'like a giant florist's azalea and altogether too much "in one's face."'*

R. 'Cynthia' may boast an AGM but in itself is not beyond criticism. Somewhat prone to powdery mildew, leggy if not grown in full sun, far too large for modern gardens and exhibiting too much magenta within its deep rose-pink blossoms are but a few of the points levelled against it. It's less often used synonym 'Lord Palmerston' also invites separate comment. It is recorded that in 1864 the aforementioned former prime minister tried to seduce the Queen's lady-in-waiting (Lady Ducre), not just for the obvious reason but in an effort to improve his standing with Queen Victoria. (*The Scotsman*, 24 April 2012)

Peter and Kenneth Cox's opinions are well recorded, especially within the pages of their classic *Encyclopedia of Rhododendron Hybrids*. If anyone ever needs a true assessment of any particular hybrid, this is the place to look. Their comments are refreshingly honest and straight to the point, and there is no beating about the (rhododendron) bush – if they don't like it they just say so.

When I asked them for a specific dislike Kenneth batted first stating that he shunned *'most, if not all of the* Rhododendron *yakushimanum hybrids, which fade badly following maturity.'* R. 'Doc' was singled out as *'one of the most uninteresting "yak" hybrids for both flowers and foliage.'* He goes on to damn R. 'Pink Petticoats' for its poor root system, chlorotic hanging leaves and, in spite of its impressive flowers *'is almost useless'.* Even its raiser (Jack Lofthouse, 1966/67) now regards it to be of no more than average worth.

RHODODENDRON 'PRESIDENT ROOSEVELT' – SHOULD IT HAVE REMAINED IN HOLLAND?

Peter, in turn, chose to rail against R. 'Elsie Straver' which he finds to have wrinkled foliage tending to yellow, with an ungainly and leggy habit. Apparently, if it was not so easy to please, as a larger flowered yellow hybrid, he would gladly give it up.

The Cox duet frequently use assessments such as 'indifferent', 'useless' and 'nothing special', which can certainly cut through any feelings of doubt one might have.

Although R. 'Nobleanum' is accepted as being welcome for its winter flowering habit, they go on to state that *'the flowers are usually of a standard which would mean an instant relegation to the bonfire if they opened in May or June.'*

To this I would will be tempted to add R. 'Christmas Cheer' for similar reasons. Its rather wishy-washy pink flowers are only of real value for their early appearance and rarely, if ever, mature in time for Christmas. All things considered I'm inclined to suggest that if Scrooge was a rhododendron fan he would surely have muttered 'humbug'.

Mark Flanagan, Keeper of the Gardens at Windsor Great Park and holder of a National Collection of Rhododendrons, was an obvious candidate to approach for an opinion. At first he asked for time to mull things over and then surprised me a little by

stating that *'if pushed, I would nominate the familiar* R. *'Sappho'. Exaggerated blotching doesn't chime with me and mature plants become leggy and open. As with most hardy hybrids the foliage is dull and uninteresting, so, sorry Mr Waterer, but your plant should have stayed in the 19th century where it was most appropriate.'* No doubt the same opinion could be directed towards R. 'Hyperion' – another of the Waterers' – which has the 'exaggerated blotch' (and regrettably, all the other negative attributes).

A nurseryman friend of mine suggested I might add R. 'Unique Marmalade' to the list. At the time I knew nothing about it, other than the very name gave cause for misgivings. According to those who know it, the general consensus would seem to be 'a bit too much', 'too fierce' and a 'bit of a loudmouth.' Obviously the marmalade is of the coarse cut variety!

John Anderson of Exbury Gardens has a definite aversion to R. 'Walloper'. The very name smacks of a total lack of subtlety and John sums up his feeling in just one word: 'gross'.

There is in fact a Walloper Group amongst which is 'Pink Walloper' (syn. 'Lem's Monarch'), 'Point Defiance' and 'Gwen Bell' all characterised by enormous trusses. Which particular one John has selected from the

Walloper Group for his vitriol is unclear; perhaps he feels the same about them all!

Although ridicule is hardly fair when one appraises R. 'Aksel Olsen' (syn. 'Axel Olson') it is a contender for eccentricity if only for its rather erratic habit of growth. Many dwarf reds have been named from Hobbie's cross of R. 'Essex Scarlet' with R. forrestii Repens Group and this clone is not considered to be, by any means, the best. The flowers and foliage deserve little criticism but the habit is definitely idiosyncratic. The Coxes state that the *'habit is rather uneven and untidy, with both vertical and horizontal branches making a bush seem to be a mounder and a spreader at the same time.'* In spite of this, or maybe because of this, seeming lack of direction, I have it in our garden and enjoy its individuality.

R. 'Wine and Roses' is another hybrid which falls short of the mark regarding floristic merit. Its excellent foliage, deep green above and superbly maroon-coloured beneath, is let down by medium, rose-coloured flowers which fade all too quickly to a washed out pink; a classic example of the term 'better to travel than to arrive'. Having stated as much, I do feel that it more than earns its place as a first rate foliage plant.

Here we should perhaps move on to some rhododendrons named in honour of famous people. One would like to feel that they all do credit to those whose name they celebrate but unfortunately that is not always the case.

Let's start with R. 'Genghis Khan' as we might assume that a plant boasting the name of a great Mongol leader who conquered the largest empire ever seen (including Afghanistan) would be as tough as old boots, but not a bit of it. Literature tells us that it is subject to weather damage, has rather weak foliage and – best of all – only gives of its best in a protected site!

R. 'Kublai Khan', named after his somewhat less ruthless grandson, should on the face of it be another tough customer but again we discover otherwise as it has yellowish, chlorotic foliage and to give of its best requires very favourable conditions.

One would have hoped that R. 'Louis Pasteur', named after the father of modern bacteriology, would be worthy of his name but also not so. As usual, the Coxes get straight to the point stating that, although floristically good it is let down by *'an appalling, straggly, vigorous upright habit which is impossible to control.'*

R. 'Humboldt' actually does due credit to the memory of that great German naturalist, but the same cannot be said for R. 'Tensing'. This was named by Wisley (where it was raised) in 1953 just after the great Sherpa, along with Sir Edmund Hillary, first climbed Mount Everest. Sadly, it is hardly worthy of the man who came from a mountain land of many fine native rhododendrons, although its orange tinted camellia-rose flowers do pass muster. These are unfortunately let down by average foliage on a very straggly plant. Sorry Wisley but the name should have gone to a finer hybrid.

Rhododendron 'Roza Stevenson', named after one of the most knowledgeable rhododendron enthusiasts of her day, barely makes the grade. This hybrid has only average foliage, with a tendency for chlorosis. In other ways it is a good plant but someone with the name Roza Stevenson deserved a result which attracts the word 'excellent'. As it was raised by John Barr and Roza Stevenson, perhaps they only have themselves to blame for not being more discriminating!

RHODODENDRON 'GINA LOLLABRIGIDA' – *MAMA MIA!* WHAT A BEAUTY!   PLANTPHOTOS.NET

Inevitably *R.* 'President Roosevelt' comes into the picture; what the great American politician did to have his name attributed to such a plant is beyond imagination. Possibly a sport of *R.* 'Limbatum' and found in Holland, many believe it should have stayed there. This variegated *R. arboreum* hybrid has a reputation for reversion and exhibits floppy little branches which snap off all too readily; it also has a tendency to unhelpfully break off at the root ball. In spite of this, it is reported to be very popular in Japan; each to his own, I suppose.

When I mentioned this hybrid to our illustrious editor she immediately stated that if one was to invite signatures from all those repelled by it, we would probably have enough to present a petition to 10 Downing Street. The comparably variegated *R.* 'Goldflimmer' attracts similar comment and is further damned by its smaller, less showy purple flowers.

The rose-pink fully domed trusses of *R.* 'Queen Mary' which was raised by Felix and Dijkhuis in 1950, is let down somewhat by its irregular habit and rather poor foliage. It has been suggested that it is best used as a background plant, but how far back, I wonder?

R. 'Gina Lollabrigida', a sister seedling of *R.* 'Queen Mary' is named in honour of the famous Italian film star and here I must plead guilty to considerable personal bias. At the height of her fame she was the apple of my (now long gone) adolescent eye and I won't have a word said against her! Literature tells us that 'Gina is good in Germany but needs protection in Denmark.' That's one way of putting it I suppose, but now is probably a good time to move on to species which demand attention.

It is all too easy to denigrate man-made hybrids rather than to point out the faults of species which, after all, are simply made the way they naturally evolved. Be that as it may, we can't let them all escape a few words of disapproval or disappointment.

Take *Rhododendron yunnanense* for instance. The beautiful clone 'Openwood' received and deserved an AGM in recognition of its high horticultural merit but one should not

HILLSIDE OF *RHODODENDRON YUNNANENSE*, FEW, IF ANY, WORTHY OF COLLECTING
MIKE ROBINSON

lose sight of the fact that not many other forms are anything like as garden worthy. Man by his very nature likes to pick and choose, and select the best. Anyone who has had the opportunity to observe *R. yunnanense* in its native haunts will have quickly realised what a variable species this is. The same may be said for other species, especially those within the Triflora Subsection, but that's by the way.

I have it on reliable authority that a recent expedition to Yunnan by members of the Royal Botanic Garden, Edinburgh became so jaundiced by the sight of so many indifferent forms of *R. yunnanense* that they decided to refer to it as *R.* yawn–anense! Having trod a similar path in Yunnan, I can but agree and it clarifies the fact that critical selection over the years has created a distorted (albeit beautiful) picture in our gardens of what is an extremely inconstant species. As the old saying goes, the Princess had to kiss a lot of frogs before she found Prince Charming!

Rhododendron invictum is a recently introduced Asian species which, by all accounts, should have been left exactly where it came from, far away on some distant Chinese hillside.

According to Kristian Theqvist, who was visiting Glendoick at the time, Peter Cox drew his visitor's attention to what he described as a not so great looking *R. invictum.* Apparently Peter stated that *'this is perhaps the most useless rhododendron that ever was or is ... flowers miserable, dirty, mouldy.'* A disparaging remark to end all disparaging remarks.

Having trekked through majestic and mature forests of *Rhododendron hodgsonii*, I am reluctant to criticise such a highly regarded Himalayan species but I feel I must draw attention to its shortcomings. Whilst I admire many of the qualities of this large leaved species – its hardiness, bold foliage, beautiful bark and eye-catching magenta flowers – I am not so keen on the actual size of the flower truss, which to my eye is not quite bold enough to match the grand proportion of the leaves. Additionally, I feel that the dark magenta flowered forms fade all too quickly to a rather grubby wishy-washy mauve. At its climax it is truly superb but the fading really marks it down.

The fact that the best form put before Committee has so far been 'Poet's Lawn' (AM 1965) and no others have been worthy of a FCC or the coveted AGM surely underlines this argument.

RHODODENDRON WIGHTII – **LOP SIDED IS AN UNDERSTATEMENT!**   JOHN MCQUIRE

R. wightii is, to put it mildly, a bit of a mystery. More than a few specialists consider the plant in general cultivation is not the true species but, as the wild collections prove near-impossible to grow in cultivation, the probable hybrid 'imposter' continues to grace our gardens, commerce and the flower shows. 'Grace' is possibly too generous a word as it does not really lend itself to being displayed in a vase. The plant itself has a very leggy, open lax habit and the flowers are presented in an extremely unbalanced one-sided truss. A one-sided truss not only looks ungainly on the show bench, it also sounds most uncomfortable!

REFERENCE ■ Cox, PA and Cox, KNE. *Encyclopedia of Rhododendron Hybrids*, Batsford, London, (1988).

RHODODENDRON HODGSONII – **RELUCTANTLY CRITICISED**   MIKE ROBINSON

Tony Schilling VMH

was Curator of Wakehurst Place, Sussex from 1967–1991 and now delights in gardening amidst the majestic mountain landscape of northwest Scotland

Return to Chongqing, Guizhou and Guangxi

PETER COX VMH

THE DRAMATIC SCENERY OF DAYAO SHAN

STEVE HOOTMAN

SEVERAL PEOPLE HAVE NOW VISITED areas to the south and east of the well-known plant hunting regions of Yunnan and Sichuan and although there are far fewer species of *Rhododendron* in particular, several have proved to be very worthwhile introductions. Four of us – Steve Hootman, Philip Evans, Peter Hutchison and myself – made our first visit to these little known districts in March and April 2009. This was the occasion when Steve had a very unfortunate injury, spiking his eye on a cut stem of bamboo, and had to go straight home for treatment. (*See Rhododendrons, Camellias and Magnolias 2010*, page 33: 'The "Five Shans Expedition" to southwest China 2009' by Philip Evans.) As a result, Steve missed half of the trip and so was very anxious to make good at the first opportunity – the following year, as it happened.

I thought this was too good a chance to miss: the opportunity to see the same very interesting areas again and perhaps some different ones, in the autumn instead of spring, was irresis-tible. Philip and Peter were unable to come but Steve brought along three other Americans: Dr Keith White of Oregon and the now married couple Kelly Dodson and Sue Milliken, owners of Far Reaches Nursery in the state of Washington. They proved to be excellent and knowledgeable companions. We were again

RHODODENDRON CHANGII ON JINFO SHAN
STEVE HOOTMAN

fortunate in having Gary Luo to organise everything for us and the expert driver Mr Liu Jun plus a new driver Mr Xieu who was very good at keeping up with Mr Liu.

In 2009 we had started in the south, in the province of Guangxi, and then gradually worked our way north, to what used to be southern Sichuan but is now included in the greater Chongqing province. As we thought the season for ripening would be more advanced in the colder north, we reversed the trip by starting in Chongqing, at the now several times visited Jinfo Shan, with its startling peaks and cliffs. In 2009 the west entrance was closed for repairs to the cable car but now it had opened again. Ten years earlier still, in 1999, Peter Hutchison and I had seen a cable car being used for transporting materials up for the construction of a new hotel and other infrastructure but the surrounds had now changed to such an extent I could not recognise if this was the same cable car site or not, nor could I find the big cave we had explored nearby.

Sadly, we only had a short time here before having to get back to the 'monkey' hotel we had stayed at the previous year, so we did not

achieve much and, as is often the case on Jinfo, visibility was poor. The hundred or so monkeys were about in force and put on a good show when fed, the bad-tempered alpha male ruling the roost.

Next day, 29th October, we were at the north entrance which we had gone to in 2009, again with a cable car. Nearing the top we saw what we thought were white flowers but soon realised it was a light coating of snow, and cold it proved to be. Quite a clear morning turned into poor visibility once again, but we made our way back to the 'Stone Forest', which covers quite an area, and we spent the best part of the day here.

There seems to be little doubt that Jinfo was once covered by good forest; now there are few trees of any size, though a lot of the rhododendrons, such as *Rhododendron coeloneuron*, have grown into substantial specimens, in this case to around 10m. Despite the constant mist for most of the year, there is a very noticeable lack of regeneration, so the rhododendrons that are endemic to this mountain, *R. platypodum* and *R. changii*, must be classed as threatened with extinction. At the time when there was good forest on Jinfo Shan, there would have been much more leaf fall and moss, the latter being the favourite medium for germination. Conservation is not helped by the efforts of the

RETURN TO
CHONGQING 2010
1. JINFO SHAN
2. JIUCAIPING SHAN
3. FANJING SHAN
4. LEIGONG SHAN
5. DAMING SHAN
6. DAYAO SHAN

Chengdu

CHONGQING

SICHUAN   Nanchuan 1

Daozhen

3

HUNAN

Zunyi

2   Kaili   4

GUIZHOU   Leishan

Guilin

YUNNAN

Lai Bin 6

5

GUANGXI

GUANGDONG

VIETNAM

RHODODENDRON PLATYPODUM CH9003,
flowering for the first time at Glendoick

PETER COX

park authorities who keep attempting to move mature specimens from the existing forest into cleared areas where there is little organic matter and full exposure. We found a recently bulldozed area with huge, newly transplanted rhododendrons in the last throws of life, planted far too deep with no hope of re-establishing. Others were planted on mounds and might struggle on for a few more years. (We had seen our first truss on *R. platypodum* at Glendoick in 2011, a fine pink.)

We now drove some distance into west Guizhou, to a peak called Jiucaiping Shan, said to be the highest in the province. This is near where we went in northeast Yunnan in 1995, and indeed this peak turned out to be as bare of woody vegetation as the peak we saw then. There were pockets of *Berberis*, *Cotoneaster* and *Osmanthus delavayi* but nearing the top we found a totally unexpected *Rhododendron*

species, closest to *R. rubiginosum* or *R. polylepis* but with whiskery bud scales. This is a long way from known populations of both these two species.

Right at the top was a second rhododendron, this one similar or identical to the *R. decorum* aff. we collected in northeast Yunnan, and which we have been calling *R. decorum* var. *cordatum* although the plant does not totally follow the description, which has a short petiole. Steve thinks this might be what the Chinese are now calling *R. nymphaeoides*.

On the way to the Bailidujian Reserve (meaning 100 Li Rhododendrons, Li being a Chinese distance measurement), also in west Guizhou, I suddenly thought I saw an ordinary *R. decorum* and shouted to the driver 'ting' (stop). It was an ordinary *R. decorum* but what I had failed to notice from the vehicle was an intriguing variety of apparent natural hybrids. The first plant seemed to be a member of subsection Triflora and then Steve shouted that he had found a typical *R. racemosum*. From then on we found apparent hybrids between these two, all varying considerably. Steve thought these might fit *R. hemitrichotum* but after further thoughts we were not so sure. This was obviously a long disturbed site, with any forest destroyed many years ago; this invariably leads to a much higher ratio of natural hybrids than occurs in virgin forest. Also growing amongst this scrub was *Photinia (Stranvaesia) davidiana* aff. with shorter leaves and brighter than usual red fruit. To my surprise, we later saw this species almost everywhere we went, along with the evergreen *Viburnum cylindricum*.

In 1999 Peter Hutchison and I had briefly visited the 100 Li Rhododendron Park and been disappointed in what we found: a litter-strewn patch of *R. arboreum* ssp. *delavayi*, *R. decorum* (in flower), *R. irroratum* and hybrids between them, sometimes called *R. x agastum*. This time we went to two different areas some distance further east. The first place had indeed almost solid rhododendrons but they were all *R. irroratum*, *R. arboreum* ssp. *delavayi* and, again, a mass of hybrids, which, from posters, showed a great range of pink shades. In a clearing was a substantial planting of young rhododendrons, obviously grown from seed, presumably wild collected. Some were growing

NEWLY TRANSPLANTED MATURE PLANTS OF
RHODODENDRON CALOPHYTUM **ON JINFO SHAN**
STEVE HOOTMAN

reasonably well and included *R. glanduliferum* (I think greatly threatened in the wild) and *R. annae* (probably also threatened), other species and some Tsutsusi azalea cultivars. The second place had, in addition to the above wild plants, two species of Tsutsusi including one growing up to 3m, with large soft leaves and an unknown species of Triflora.

We now ventured northeast to the peak of Fanjing Shan, well described by Philip in the 2010 Yearbook. We travelled up together in one of the open minibuses, as we had the previous year. I walked down, as I did then, the others went right to the top.

There is now a cable car on the opposite side from the road to the top, presumably near where the steps are that Jim Russell had to tackle in 1986 when there was no other way. In 2009 we had found a species of subsection Triflora and perhaps failed to look at it properly and assumed that *Rhododendrons of China vol. 2* were correct in calling this *R. ambiguum*. On examining it more carefully, we came to the conclusion that this is not the above but probably a species nova as the scales on the leaf underside are all wrong. Otherwise we saw all the same species recorded in the previous year. In the morning Sue and I walked down the road from the hotel while the others went back up the road intending to walk some way down from there. We found *R. ovatum* and *R. mariesii*, making a total of fifteen species on the mountain, good for this part of China.

All our party are keen on the family *Araliaceae*, so when Sue and I found one plant of a neat little evergreen species, (and another found later on Leigong Shan), it received our 'plant of the day' award.

Our next mountain was Leigong Shan, which we also visited in 2009, and we started here by driving right to the top. It soon became apparent that very few plants had set seed and there was evidence of severe spring frosts which had even caused bark split on several plants. All the magnolias seemed to be devoid of fruit as did most members of the family *Styracaceae*. Fortunately, the many plants of *Rhododendron fortunei* near the top did not appear to be suffering from scale insects to the extent they were in 2009.

Perhaps a case of a coincidence but strange all the same, Steve's eye that he had damaged here the previous year started to flare up again. It was great having Dr Keith with us to administer treatment to the eye and thankfully, it greatly improved as soon as we left the offending mountain.

BARK SPLIT ON *RHODODENDRON COELONEURON*
ON LEIGONG SHAN   STEVE HOOTMAN

Note was made in 2009 of an attractive flaking barked species of *Clethra* but this year we noticed that there are, in fact, two species here, the other with a rough bark. The former had shed most of its capsules while the latter was still laden, which would indicate that they flower at different times of the year. The classification of *Clethra* seems to be in some disarray, with the Flora of China giving *C. monostachya* and *C. cavalierei* both as synonyms of *C. delavayi* and adding the following: *C. bodinieri, C. fabri, C. petelotii* and *C. kaipoensis* so we do not know at this stage what species we found, especially as we did not see them in leaf or flower in 2009 or 2010.

As in 2009, we found just three plants of *Rhododendron glanduliferum* here, underlying its rarity, and we re-encountered the big patch of *Cardiocrinum giganteum* var. *yunnanense*, many of which had flowered.

Being a Saturday, it was very obvious that these now accessible peaks draw many Chinese tourists. On the whole this is a good thing, but there is evidence that they are liable to pick much of what is in flower within easy reach of the track. Gary told us that during the Chinese May holiday, there are huge crowds, all accommodation is full and it is wise for foreigners to avoid these peak times.

This was another beautiful warm sunny day, a state of affairs which continued to the end of our trip. I had hoped that we would see some good autumn colour but found this disappointing with only a very few trees and shrubs colouring well. Nevertheless, I would still recommend mid to late autumn as a good time to visit much of China.

(One thing I would never do in China is to drive any type of vehicle. The Chinese have a completely different way of driving to us. They obviously think that to drive at the best of their ability they have to avoid other vehicles (and people) by inches rather than the several feet which most of us do. This not only applies to oncoming vehicles or going through a gap with an inch on each side to spare, but in towns they drive right up to the bumper of another vehicle in front, leaving just an inch or two gap between. They have a lot to learn about motorways too, with apparently no rules about which side of the road slow vehicles should use or which side to pass on. Each trip I have been on in China I have experienced some incredibly near misses; this time a motorbike coming straight for us on the wrong side of the road around a bend. How we missed each other I will never know. Anyone that feels nervous at being driven should not go to China!)

We walked a long way down the road right to the Leigong Shan park entrance taking notice of several genera among which was a fine plant of the most attractive hornbeam *Carpinus fangiana*, with its large rugose leaves and conspicuous pendulous catkins, a recent introduction to cultivation. There were many plants of section Choniastrum of *Rhododendron*, which we had seen in flower the previous year but again there was little sign on most of them as having flowered this year.

Like the *Clethra* earlier, here I became rather confused over *Enkianthus* species. The previous year we had seen masses of the beautiful white flowered *E. serrulatus* on several of the peaks we visited and noticed no other. This year there seemed to be two species, the above with larger leaves and capsules and another with smaller leaves and capsules, probably *E. chinensis*.

FAGUS IN AUTUMN COLOUR ON LEIGONG SHAN
STEVE HOOTMAN

***CARPINUS FANGIANA* ON LEIGONG SHAN**
STEVE HOOTMAN

That was the end of our travels in Guizhou and we now drove southwards into Guangxi. As Gary had been refused permits twice for us to explore Maoer Shan, the authorities saying that no foreigners are allowed in, we thought we would try the neighbouring Huaping Shan which might have a similar flora. Reaching the gate, they were again reluctant to let us in, so as a last resort, Gary rang the director but with no success. This meant that we would not be able to see the endemic *Rhododendron* species, notably *R. yuefengense* which is proving such a success in cultivation, and the other species of subsection Fortunea, *R. maoerense*. Further species that had been found on Maoer Shan were *R. levinei*, *R. orbiculare* ssp. *cardiobasis* and *R. oligocarpum*; the first two we were to see on Dayao Shan, the last on Fanjing Shan.

(Each city we came to after dark was lit up with flashing or non-flashing neon lights; some being quite artistic, others more garish. Thinking back to my first visit to China over thirty years ago, I could never possibly have imagined how much things would change in those comparatively few years. It is the cities and roads that have made such a startling transformation. Much of the country has barely changed, with the same labour intensive production of crops and the same hovels that many of these labourers still live in. Young people, seeing the good life in the cities, are flocking there hoping to escape the manual drudgery their forebears had to suffer, although in the end, perhaps, they might have led happier lives still tilling the soil. The contrast between rich and poor is getting wider and wider which is beginning to ferment a lot of trouble for the authorities.)

We now had a long drive to investigate Daming Shan, away southwestwards towards the Vietnam frontier. To our knowledge, no westerners had ever been there or at least not in recent years. This caused a lengthy heated argument between Gary and Mr Liu. Apparently, Mr Liu was responsible for paying road tolls and for fuel after an initial agreement was arranged on how much the overall mileage was likely to cost. What we were planning was obviously extra mileage over and above what was originally estimated but somehow, thankfully, all was amicably settled. During this drive we crossed the Tropic of Cancer and, as a consequence, the local roadside trees and plantations changed dramatically. Roadside trees were largely a combination of *Eucalyptus* and *Bauhinia*, the latter still in full flower,

***RHODODENDRON FAITHIAE* ON DAMING SHAN**
STEVE HOOTMAN

varying from deep pink to white and very attractive. Neat *Eucalyptus* plantations covered much of the hilly ground with sugar cane on the flat, probably destined for bio fuel.

Daming Shan is another of these steep sided mountains with a near flat top; it is no great altitude but its isolation means endemic or near endemic species. The height we recorded was only 1,350m but the flora at that altitude is largely temperate. As before, we were able to drive to the top and very soon found what we were looking for: *Rhododendron faithiae* and *R. wumingense* which thrilled both Steve and me. The former is a member of subsection Fortunea with large wide leaves, the latter is at present classified as a Maddenia but looked to us very similar to *R. moupinense*. Neither proved to be all that common, especially *R. wumingense*, the biggest I saw being about 1.2m both ways. It has attractive elongated red flower buds and one to two flowers per inflorescence. Poor *R. faithae* was being devoured by different species of hairy caterpillars, still very active on the 10th of November. In many cases there was nothing left but the midrib and even some of these had

RHODODENDRON WUMINGENSE ON DAMING SHAN   STEVE HOOTMAN

gone so far that this year's leaves were already falling off, making the plants like a skeleton. Nature can be cruel. The biggest I saw was nearly 4m. high. The question is: Will these species be hardy? I think they will as it is amazing what is proving hardy from Vietnam, and not necessarily from the highest peaks. Other fine plants here were *Gordonia axillaris* (now *Polyspora axillaris*), with dark evergreen leaves and white camellia-like flowers, a very nice *Daphniphyllum* with striking red petioles and a Tsutsusi azalea with tiny leaves, probably *Rhododendron minutiflorum*.

We spent the night in the town of Lai Bin which had the largest bedding scheme I have ever seen: all along the main road was planted with different coloured foliage and corkscrew-type topiary.

Our last peak was Shengtang Shan, part of Dayao Shan, where we were in poor weather the previous year, with zero visibility. This time all was revealed, and what a mountain it is – easily rivalling Jinfo Shan, the European Dolomites or the Torres del Paine in southern Chile for drama. The various peaks surrounded the hotel in a cirque and rose up in a most striking fashion.

The terrible road up in 2009 had been transformed a year later, now with a perfect surface. Then the whole mountain had been

THE CLIFF TRACK ON DAYAO SHAN
STEVE HOOTMAN

shrouded in thick mist and apart from one fleeting glimpse in the evening, the mountain was blotted out. This time everything was clear, so off we went, again up the steps, this time dry and so much easier to negotiate, especially on the way down when they were very slippery before.

The first day we did a preliminary canter up and soon Kelly and Sue were in raptures, having found *Heteropolygonatum rosealum*, a newly described Solomon's Seal, endemic to this mountain, with its handsome thick wide leaves and large black fruit.

Large shrubs or small trees with a fine flaking bark, on close examination turned out to be a surprise *Rhododendron*, missed in the gloom of the previous year. This was *R. guihainianum*, a newly described member of subsection Fortunea, most likely tender as it was at a low altitude with a lot of mountain above it.

On our earlier visit we realised that the upper path had been cut out of the edge of a sheer cliff, with bulging rock immediately above one's head and just a feeble rail stopping one from falling into oblivion, but at the time the dense mist hid the view. This time it was all too obvious and I soon retreated, due to my vertigo horror, and while the others bravely carried on to the top, in total up some 3,600 steps, they all admitted that they were scared too. At least the

RHODODENDRON SP. NOVA (THE TRUE R. CARDIOBASIS) ON DAYAO SHAN

STEVE HOOTMAN

plants were also more easily seen and the four of them were very impressed with fine specimens of *Rhododendron simiarum*, a species of subsection Argyrophylla, wide-spread in southern China, even occurring in the Hong Kong New Territories. Steve reckoned that the Fortunea we saw a small plant of in 2009 might be *R. orbiculare* ssp. *cardiobasis*, which also grows on Maoer Shan. Plants cultivated from the latter source may have cordate bases to the leaves but otherwise show little resemblance to *R. orbiculare*. Other rhododendrons were the maddenias *R. levinei* (also seen in 2009) and *R. liliiflorum*, plus a Choniastrum, two members of Tsutsusi and *R. mariesii*, a total of nine species, not bad for a mountain of only 1,970m.

Sadly, there was still no sign of *R. dachengense*, a Taliensia that has been recently described, which presumably must occur on one of the other peaks of Dayao Shan. (Steve eventually found this in October 2012 on the third attempt on Dayao Shan.)

There are three impressive rare conifers at the higher elevations: *Fokienia hodginsii, Podocarpus wangii* and a huge spreading *Nothotsuga longibracteata*.

Amazingly, there is a hotel up at the top of those awesome steps and everything has to be carried up by porters, no wonder it is expensive.

RHODODENDRON SIMIARUM ON DAYAO SHAN

STEVE HOOTMAN

***NOTHOTSUGA LONGIBRACTEATA* ON DAYAO SHAN** STEVE HOOTMAN

I saw one elderly man staggering up with a heavy-looking load but he seemed to be quite cheerful – porters have a strong stick across their shoulders, with balancing loads hanging from each end.

We spent two nights in Guilin, preparing ourselves for the journey home and buying presents. In contrast to the previous year, Guilin was very pleasantly warm and we were able to go out to restaurants in the evenings in just our shirtsleeves.

Overall it was a good trip: fine plants, excellent company and mostly gorgeous weather. 'Plants of the trip' voted for were – a herb: a *Briggsia* species with purple flowers; a tree or shrub other than a rhododendron: the dwarf *Araliaceae* and a *Rhododendron: R. faithiae*, which was also voted the overall winner.

Peter Cox VMH

is a renowned authority on rhododendrons in cultivation and in the wild. He has written several landmark books, most recently Seeds of Adventure, *co-authored with his plant-hunting friend Peter Hutchison*

***BRIGGSIA MIHIERI* –** voted 'Plant of the Trip' in the herb category STEVE HOOTMAN

A history of rhododendrons at Tremough

SARAH BENNEY

TREMOUGH HAS LONG BEEN FAMED for the beauty and variety of its rhododendrons. William Shilson was in occupation of the Tremough estate, near Falmouth in Cornwall, from 1865 to 1875 and had a passion for gardening. It was he that adopted the Victorian craze for rhododendrons which brought Tremough to the forefront of the horticultural scene and it was one of his Head Gardeners, Richard Gill, who elevated the hybridisation of rhododendrons from a skill into an art.

As the plant hunters brought back seeds from the newly discovered specimens in the Himalayas, the fashion for rhododendrons swept the country, and estate owners vied with each other to produce ever finer varieties through hybridisation. Tremough was ideally placed for this, with its moist temperate climate and acid soils providing an ideal environment, it became famed for its rhododendron production.

It has oft been reported, as yet unproven, that William Shilson was sent a large number of seeds from Joseph Hooker's first Sikkim collection by Joseph's father, William Hooker, Director of the Royal Botanical Gardens at Kew. (Because of the time frame, it is possible that Shilson was sent seedlings to grow on.) The cultivation of these precious collections was entrusted to Tremough's Head Gardener, Richard Gill, who developed considerable skills in the culture of rhododendrons. William Shilson had always been a keen horticulturalist and regular competitor in local garden society shows, and it was entirely fitting that his greatest legacy should be the outstanding red hybrid *Rhododendron* 'Shilsonii', a glorious first cross between two Hooker collections, *R. thomsonii* and *R. barbatum* justifiably given an RHS Award of Merit in 1900.

Daniel Henry Shilson was the third son of William and Anne Shilson and became the owner of Tremough after his father's death. Anne, who stayed on at Tremough, shared her husband's interest in horticulture, and a friend's gift to her of a particularly good form of *R. griffithianum* from the Italian lakes made a valuable contribution to the hybridisation programme. Daniel maintained the association with the Royal Botanical Gardens at Kew through his donation of a huge consignment of Himalayan rhododendrons to be planted in Kew's new Temperate House. The selection comprised a wide variety of specimens including a large specimen of *R.* 'Shilsonii'. These flourished in the Temperate House for many years but eventually grew too large and they were finally transferred to the RHS garden at Wisley.

A FINE GROUP OF RHODODENDRONS AT THE FRONT OF THE HOUSE AT TREMOUGH   CLAUDIO PAVANA

Richard Gill was a talented hybridiser of rhododendrons and worked on Hooker's recently discovered Himalayan species to produce a number of outstanding varieties, and together with his family he was to acquire a worldwide reputation. Gill's list of 'New and noteworthy hybrid Rhododendrons of own raising' included forty varieties, many of which won acclaim from the RHS. Richard Gill was particularly proud of R. 'Gill's Gloriosum', which had massive pyramidal trusses of clear pink flowers and in 1925 also received an RHS Award of Merit. He commented *'It is considered by many to be the finest Rhododendron ever raised.'* R. 'Gill's Goliath' was another form, with enormous soft pink flowers, and other successful varieties included R. 'Duke of Cornwall' (*arboreum* x *barbatum*) AM 1907; R. 'Ernest Gill' (*arboreum* x *fortunei*) AM 1918; R. 'Delight' AM 1929; R. 'Fireball' AM 1925; R. 'Trelawny' AM 1936; R. 'William Watson' AM 1925. Nine of Gill's hybrids received RHS Awards of Merit. His greatest

RICHARD GILL POSES WITH ONE OF HIS RHODODENDRONS AT TREMOUGH

M E POTTER

success however, winning the coveted RHS First Class Certificate in 1902, was R. 'Beauty of Tremough' (*griffithianum* x blood red *arboreum*) AM 1893, which was a free grower with fine foliage and flowers of blush pink with a bright pink edge. Seedlings were sent to other Cornish gardens and to Sir Edmund Loder at Leonardslee. Clones of this hybrid range in colour from the white with a slight pink flush of R. 'Trebah Gem' to R. 'Gill's Triumph' with large crimson scarlet flowers. Different clones have been awarded one FCC and five AMs: one from Bodnant as recently as 1981 as R. 'Treetops'.

At one point Richard Gill was believed to hold the largest stock of hybrid rhododendrons in the world. The grounds of Tremough were planted with scores of varieties and shades; numerous examples grew to a height of 25 to 30 feet and many carried enormous flowers. Gill considered that *'such gigantic trusses as we grow must be the envy of many gentlemen.'*

Richard Gill began his career in the garden at Tremough and he was a hands-on gardener learning from working with plants rather than from books. Nevertheless, his knowledge and ability gained widespread recognition for he became a Fellow of the RHS.

Gill leased the old walled garden at Tremough to set up his nursery business from where he cultivated his most successful hybrids on a commercial basis. At the end of the lease he joined with his son and the nursery was removed to Kernick Manor, lower down the hillside but still within sight of Tremough.

Gill believed that 'thoroughness' was the key to his success. Rhododendrons needed individual care, not only during propagation, but also as mature plants if they were to be shown at their best. His favourite method of propagation was the raising of plants from seed, for species raised this way had the advantage of *'being true to their kind and of possessing robust constitution.'* As a practical man he did however recognise the advantages in time offered by budding, grafting or layering. It was Gill's considered opinion that *'Tremough ranks as the Rhododendron Garden of Cornwall and here, if anywhere, the cultivation of these beautiful plants has reached the acme of perfection…'*

Richard Ernest Gill began his horticultural career as assistant to his father Richard at Tremough. As a result of a meeting with William Watson, the Assistant Curator at Kew Gardens, he entered Kew in 1899. While there he studied geographical botany, physics, chemistry, oceanography and systematic botany and, before leaving in 1901, submitted a collection of British flora. He learned the nursery trade, before returning to Cornwall to work with his father at Kernick Manor. Here they set up the Himalayan Nurseries and erected what were thought to be the largest green-houses in the West Country. The Gills soon outgrew their 10 acres at Kernick and purchased a further 23 acres of land at Carclew where they could grow their rhodo-dendrons in a woodland setting.

The Gills' nursery consolidated its reputation as a firm of world repute, and in their catalogue they offered for sale a vast range of species and hybrids, including those produced by Richard Gill in his years at Tremough. Gill also continued his experimentation with new types and crosses, helped by a continued acquisition of new plant material from the East. The Gills received material collected by two of Richard Ernest's brothers, Herbert and Norman, both of whom held appointments in botanical gardens in India and also employed their own native plant hunters in the remote mountain regions of Tibet. The Gills' reputation led to orders from many parts of the world; rhododendrons were despatched to New Zealand, the United States, South America, Japan and Italy.

Richard Ernest Gill was acknowledged as an expert in his field and was proud to advise members of the Royal family on the planting of their estates. At horticultural shows, the Gills won outright the prestigious Rothschild Challenge Cup for trade exhibits by gaining first place on three successive occasions.

Today the rhododendrons are still the glory of the grounds at Tremough, now a University Campus, and there are currently nine gardeners,

RICHARD GILL'S GREATEST HYBRIDISING SUCCESS:
R. 'BEAUTY OF TREMOUGH' TREMOUGH ARCHIVE

led by Head Gardener David Garwood, who continue to tend them. There has been much work done in feeding and mulching, and in pruning overgrown specimens, cutting out old ponticum rootstocks and some relocation of plants that have outgrown their sites. A policy has been adopted to plant only rhododendron species from the Sikkim Himalayas or hybrids that are found in the Gill catalogues, within the old Tremough Estate.

Over the past century Gill's hybrids have become difficult to obtain and, as a valuable conservation measure, Tremough continues to work with Ros Smith from Duchy College at Rosewarne who has taken rhododendron buds to micropropagate in order to conserve this rare collection.

ACKNOWLEDGMENTS
This article is based on Margaret Grose's fine book, *Tremough, Penryn: The Historic Estate*, MH & GM Grose, (2003). I would like to thank Margaret for allowing me to use large sections for this article, as well as helping the gardening team at Tremough with valuable research.

Sarah Benney

is a gardener in the Tremough campus gardening team

Phytophthora ramorum … ten years on

IAN WRIGHT

with contributions by ROS SMITH, ANN PAYNE, CHRIS TRIMMER & FRANKLYN TANCOCK

10 YEARS have now passed since *Phytophthora ramorum* was first confirmed in the UK. What have we learnt in that time and what could the future hold for us?

First let's take a step back for those few remaining people who can consider themselves fortunate not to have come across this virulent plant disease, and just remind ourselves of the pathogen that is now very much 'at large' throughout the UK but particularly in the West.

WHAT IS *PHYTOPHTHORA RAMORUM*?

Phytophthora are fungus-like disease pathogens; they belong to a group of organisms known as oomycetes. Oomycetes were thought until recently to be fungi as they spore and have hyphae but DNA analysis in the 1990s indicated that they were more closely related to the algae groups (diatoms and brown algae in particular). They are in a separate taxonomic kingdom, part of the algae community 'Chromista', as opposed to a fungi kingdom member. Therefore *Phytophthora* are known as being 'fungal like'.

WHERE DID IT COME FROM AND WHAT HAS HAPPENED IN THE LAST 10 YEARS?

One of the first references to *Phytophthora ramorum* was along the west coast of the USA in the 1990s where a close relation of the UK strain of *Phytophthora ramorum*, had been, and is still, devastating the American Tan Oak population, along with many other species.

The disease was first noted in the UK in 2002, initially intercepted by our Plant Health Inspectors mainly on *Viburnum* and *Rhododendron* within the horticultural trade, but it quickly became apparent after initial surveys that infected plants planted out into private and public gardens had spread the disease to other susceptible species and existing mature stock. *P. ramorum* spores were found to be aerially dispersed within water particles and as

RHODODENDRONS GROWING AT THE NATIONAL TRUST PLANT CONSERVATION CENTRE

NATIONAL TRUST

the host list of affected plants grew (now amounting to over 150 species) so did our concern over the future of so many of our much loved garden taxa. Would this be the demise of growing rhododendrons as we know it, what will we do without these plants we love so much and perhaps have taken for granted as being with us forever? Most of the questions emulated from the fact that at that time our understanding and knowledge of the pathogen was sadly lagging behind the pace of change and speed that these new hosts were being confirmed, also compounded by the discovery of a new but similar *Phytophthora* later named *Phytophthora kernoviae* after the area it was first found (Cornish for Cornwall is 'kernow').

As the (now) two diseases took hold in the wetter west of the UK (climatic maps predicted these areas were of higher risk due to favourable conditions for the disease, particularly higher rainfall) and our ability to locate and identify them improved, we started to realise that our native flora could also be threatened, with some key plant species being highly susceptible. So a targeted campaign against the invasive and highly susceptible disease host *Rhododendron ponticum* began, but this came too late to protect the native heath species *Vaccinium myrtillus* (Bilberry) which was found to be highly susceptible and at great risk. As a consequence it has suffered from a number of outbreaks, particularly in Cornwall, with very limited management options within the challenging terrain.

The previous Government realised that these growing issues were going to need a large injection of new money to support better understanding via research, and more robust actions aimed at slowing the spread of this quarantine organism from its seemingly relentless march through natural and heritage environments, not forgetting the impacts and costs that the UK's nursery industry affected by the disease were having to bear alone.

In the spring of 2009 a further £25 million of new funding support was agreed and a 5 year programme commenced to: slow the spread of the disease, protect heathlands and other valuable plant communities, improve our understanding and provide us with management options.

Part of these new funds were directed towards increasing the numbers of Plant Health Inspectors available to survey and take action against the disease and support affected owners if the pathogen was confirmed present on their site.

It should be remembered that *P. ramorum* (also *P. kernoviae*) continue to be notifiable diseases covered by specific legislation under the Plant Health Act and, specific to *Phytophthora ramorum*, the Plant Health Order 2004 (England) and (Forestry 2005)

aimed to prevent the spread of this harmful organism. This means there is an obligation to take action if found; no action is still not an option.

It was perhaps inevitable that more trained eyes surveying would mean more outbreaks confirmed, so numbers of hosts and new outbreaks continued to rise.

Then a real step change of the worst kind occurred in 2009 when a number of dead and dying Japanese Larch (*Larix kaempferi*) were found in the South West, and once the difficult task of isolating the pathogen was overcome, *Phytophthora ramorum* was eventually confirmed to be the cause. This was a very worrying development because it meant that we had a tree which was both highly susceptible and a major sporulating host. This meant that long distance spore dispersal was quite possible and that *P. ramorum* had in effect created a full circle from nurseries into gardens into the natural environment which then threatened nurseries. By this time the nurseries had less incidence of the disease because of fewer interceptions; this was due to better practice, awareness and restrictions on known high risk trade pathways reducing interception figures in the trade to as low as 0.2 % of all targeted inspections recently reported.

Why did it take so long for larch to become affected? Among many theories, one is that weather events such as rainfall and wind in the preceding years allowed a build-up of inoculum to reach levels which could trigger tree-to-tree spread via spore distribution without the aid of any man-made pathways of within 100m locally to between 1–3km from infected stands of trees. After some rather rapid research focussed on larch it was found that a single infected larch needle could have as many as 2000 spores, each capable of releasing around 10 zoospores, each of these capable of starting a new outbreak. To put this into context a *Rhododendron ponticum* leaf with a $4cm^2$ lesion can produce 8 sporangia, each containing perhaps 8–10 zoospores, each of these capable of starting a new infection. To date the losses of larch are quite significant and it was estimated that over 3 million larch trees had been felled or placed under statutory notice by the end of 2011 in England and Wales alone. The situation is very much ongoing as this goes to print. The Forestry commission (FC) working with the Food and Environment Research agency (FERA) are applying a strict policy of control measures in an attempt to slow down the speed of distribution, in that all host trees within a 150m radius of the infected tree are felled and any timber then needing extracting will need to satisfy biosecurity protocols, as will the processing facilities licensed to accept infected material. The key then is to ensure this material cannot re-enter the horticulture industry as a growing medium or mulch which might then cause new outbreaks.

The economic cost of a major disease outbreak such as *Phytophthora ramorum* is hard to quantify, but in an estimate prior to its discovery on Larch, Defra placed the full economic impact on the UK between £20 million and £30 million (Defra, 2008). In the National Trust alone the direct cost to the organisation since 2005 is around £1million.

This all sounds a little bleak when first read, but I do think we have a much better understanding about how we might live with *P. ramorum*. I am prepared to be challenged in my personal view that a magic cure will not appear, at least not yet, for *P. ramorum*, it now being too widespread. However *P. kernoviae* is still fairly confined, always remembering that any disease that has escaped outside of the confines of a nursery or glasshouse becomes a very difficult if not impossible challenge to eradicate, especially one that can produce such long-lasting survival spores (chalamaedospores) as *P. ramorum* can; such spores are thought to have a dormancy lifespan in excess of 5 years.

LESSONS LEARNED

When we challenged the way we manage our gardens it quickly became apparent that our plant records were far from perfect, and that our garden management lacked basic hygiene and good husbandry – especially evident when resources become stretched.

The National Trust committed (with support in the form of sponsorship from Yorkshire and Clydesdale Bank) to survey, map and record our most valuable plant collections, developing a new, user-friendly database for our garden teams. The objective of this was to gain a better understanding of which plants were threatened or needing safeguarding via propagation.

PLANT SURVEYS & *PHYTOPHTHORA*

The undertaking of plant surveys within the National Trust's garden and parks over the past five years was initially to discover what we owned, such knowledge would give us a better understanding of how to best maintain and safeguard the collection, which is considered one of the biggest, if not *the* biggest under single ownership. But with the onslaught from the threat of *Phytophthora* and other diseases it soon become apparent that this would also be a way of knowing what our resources are for working and coping with the threat of such natural adversities.

To date we have surveyed almost half of the properties within our care; thankfully this includes most of those with major plant collections. The task has been challenging and a steep learning curve for all concerned but fortunately we have been able to adjust and adapt the methodology as appropriate when new issues occurred. If individual properties haven't the resources available to undertake the survey work themselves, we have built up a strong team of experienced professionals within the organisation to take on the work; they fully understand the tasks and their importance towards plant conservation.

Surveying and mapping a plant collection usually results in a good baseline on which to build future records, however, gardens with more significant collections of rhododendrons, such as Rowallane, Mount Stewart, Trengwainton and Bodnant, all needed a more expert eye to analyse the data and provide a clearer picture of which plants should receive priority attention.

For one property, under the imminent threat of *Phytophthora* in its tree canopy, we adapted the GPS recording form to allow for extra information to be added which would give us a better picture of our immediate conservation requirement should the worst happen. The extra data recorded included the current health condition of the plants, the impact from the removal of the offending trees including the

THE NATIONAL TRUST PLANT CONSERVATION CENTRE, relocated during 2012 to a new biosecure site

NATIONAL TRUST

root plates and the plant's value in the wider picture of plant conservation. The other, and perhaps the most important information gathered, was judging whether the plant would survive in its new micro-climate once the canopy was removed.

Developing and tailoring these skills means we are now in a better position to manage the conservation needs of our plant collection by knowing the locations of vulnerable subjects. We can now implement a propagation programme which will enable us to perpetuate threatened subjects in more suitable areas of the country which have escaped or are less susceptible to the threat from *Phytophthora* etc. We accept that some subjects run the risk of being lost for ever but at least we will know that we did the best we could and have a detailed knowledge of their existence.

HOW DO WE SAVE OUR GARDENS' PLANT HERITAGE?

This was one of the questions we asked ourselves and in response to the difficulties posed by plant movement restrictions on an infected site we've had to become more inventive in finding appropriate solutions.

The National Trust's own Plant Conservation Centre took on the challenge even when local *Phytophthora ramorum* issues made it a necessity to move the whole operation to a new, more biosecure site, away from a garden and highly susceptible trees that might put these highly valuable plants at risk.

As part of the survey process we often use a conservation flow chart as a method of assessing a plant's conservation value and giving it a score that would steer the urgency of any propagation requirement.

However, if a garden is under a Plant Health Notice preventing the spread of *P. ramorum*, we require written permission from the Food and Environment Research Agency before moving any material from site; if the plant is infected or near infection, safeguarding via propagation is a significant challenge at the least.

Our first port of call especially for rhododendrons is Ros Smith based at Duchy College, Camborne in Cornwall and the micropropagation facility Ros runs is still the only FERA-licensed facility to process infected material.

MICROPROPAGATION OF RHODODENDRONS

There has been considerable success after building up extensive knowledge through experience of the many pitfalls in trying to get this material to respond. The conservation programme has been focussing on historic and rare rhododendrons under threat by age, disease and climatic stresses.

Started in 2005 in order to conserve historic rhododendrons in Cornish gardens, the technique used involves the laboratory production of tiny plantlets from small pieces of plant material, such as vegetative buds and shoots and floral buds too. This is done initially by using a dilute solution of bleach then, by successive selection, the resulting plantlets are cleaned of *Phytophthora*. These are grown in a nutrient jelly with added plant growth hormones which allows manipulation of the way that plants grow.

RHODODENDRON 'MORVAH' (BOLITHO HYBRID) EX DUCHY MICROPROP c.5 YEARS OLD. Planted as part of an ADAS/FERA trial at a Cornish garden in an area which had known *P. ramorum* positive plants. Note the viburnum, which had been identified as *P. ramorum* positive and now in severe decline. Could the increased vigour ex-microprop provide the rhododendron with increased resistance to *ramorum*?

NATIONAL TRUST

Plantlets are returned to the National Trust Plant Conservation Centre (PCC) in Devon at the rooting stage, for acclimatisation and growing on; other organisations can receive them at a later stage of development. Although many plants are produced from a small amount of material, it takes a minimum of two years to produce rooted plantlets. Over 900 rhododendron species and cultivars are being or have been micropropagated since the programme began, sent from 37 gardens, parks and arboreta around the UK. The success rate is around 95% but could be higher if floral buds are collected at the best stage of development. It is known that at least ten of the mother plants are no longer alive and many others will have been rescued from certain loss. There is great satisfaction in returning micropropagated plantlets following the receipt, through the post, of an almost dead twig with the accompanying note 'This was all that was left, it was cut down and put on the bonfire before we realised it was important!'

Magnolias and camellias are among other susceptible plants that can be micropropagated; however research is ongoing to produce rooted plantlets at the final stage of propagation; it is so frustrating to have shoots which will not initiate roots, though it is only a matter of time.

THE NATIONAL TRUST PLANT CONSERVATION CENTRE (PCC) – AFTERCARE

Once Ros has worked her magic in the lab it's down to the PCC to gradually wean the new plantlets off from the agar gel and into compost. This we do by gently washing the agar from the roots and potting up individually into 6cm pots which are then placed into a sealed cabinet to mimic the conditions they were growing in. Gradually we allow more and more air whilst still misting overhead, until the lid is taken completely off. After a period of about 6 months we pot them into a 1ltr air pot (www.superoots.com/) where they are grown on in a shade tunnel until being moved into a 3ltr air pot, cut back and then placed onto our drip system where the water uptake is regulated. This whole process can take a minimum of 4 years to complete but at the end a slice of our country's plant heritage has been saved for future generations to enjoy. Some of our most precious rhododendrons from Cornish gardens have been rescued in this way, for example *Rhododendron macabeanum*; this was the original Frank Kingdon-Ward plant that flowered for the first time in this country. Prioritised due to its unique plant heritage it was one of the first to be saved in this way and has now been spread to other gardens to help safeguard its future.

WITH A GARDEN UNDER RESTRICTIONS, WHAT HAPPENS TO OTHER GENERA WHICH NEED PROPAGATION?

This is where we move our propagation expertise onto site, the first port of call being our plants' database to check which plants are important; from then on it can be a race against time to propagate plants before they die or are destroyed.

We know we cannot move the young plants from an infected site but the hope is that they may be more resilient to re-infection, or at least can be planted out after all other host plants have been removed; unfortunately this is the only option open to us until we get a negative result for *Phytophthora* from the site.

We propagate by seed, cuttings or, in the case of *Magnolia*, grafting on a hot-pipe system. Generally speaking we use either a *M. campbellii* or *M. kobus* rootstock depending on requirements; due to the nature of the plants we deal with it's not always possible to propagate from the best material.

This is what makes it more rewarding when you have success, the resulting new plant may not look like a 'cat walk model' but it has potential and any resulting new growth will be re-propagated to produce a plant that is worthy of being planted out.

Success has been achieved in this way at various sites in the southwest; any equipment we set up on an infected site will then stay there for future use.

PRACTICAL ACTIONS

During the last few years the term 'biosecurity' has become part of new vocabulary within our gardens and synonymous with preventing the entry or spread of diseases such *P. ramorum*. This term covers a whole range of aspects of garden management from *sensible* purchasing to general good husbandry and hygiene; healthy plants are less likely to succumb to disease, therefore good cultural husbandry such as trying to match a plant to its preferred location, soil type and conditions is likely to help.

Avoiding planting into previously infected areas is a requirement of a Statutory Plant Health Notice: 'no susceptible plant is to be planted within 3m of an infected plant for 4 years.' Having *Phytophthora ramorum* confirmed means you need to understand how plants might become infected by spores remaining in or on the soil, for example, one pathway might be lower leaves in contact with soil or rain splash, therefore measures such as removing the lower leaves or mulching around the plant to prevent soil splashing on to leaves may help.

Planting with sufficient space around is also essential to ensure good air movement so that humidity, which this pathogen thrives on, is reduced.

Throughout the last seven years there has been a targeted campaign against *Rhododendron ponticum*, the reason being that it is known to be a highly susceptible sporulating host of both *Phytophthora ramorum* and *Phytophthora kernoviae*. In total, 600 hectares have been cleared in the UK; many would say that this has a double benefit due to the invasive habit *R. ponticum* displays in certain situations .

Something we can all do is to improve garden hygiene since pests and pathogens are readily spread around a garden on soil and plant debris attached to footwear, tools (e.g. pruning knives, secateurs, saws etc.) or on tractors and other vehicles or machinery. Keeping paths well-drained and clear of soil and plant debris will also slow the movement of diseases around a site.

Our gardens have a limited palette of chemicals to play with these days partly due to our commitment to more greener practices, but we in the NT recommend the use of products such as 'Jet 5' which is recommended for general purpose disinfectant tasks, or 'Cleankill Sanitising Spray' which helps to form a barrier against pathogens such as *P. ramorum*.

Poor irrigation and watering practice will also provide pathways for disease so if possible use a source of water that is free from pests and diseases. But if water is collected on-site, ideally it should be treated in some way to destroy pathogens. Methods might include, for larger sites and nurseries, slow sand filtration – this has been proved to be completely effective at removing pathogens such as *Phytophthora* species (including *P. ramorum*) from water. However, it is expensive. Alternative cheaper systems include ultra-violet light, chlorination or ozone.

Dealing with plant waste in a sensible manner is another weapon against the spread of *Phytophthora*. Ideally, plant waste should be collected and kept secure prior to disposal and not subject to dispersal during windy conditions. Acceptable methods of disposal include composting, burning and, although not very eco-friendly, deep burial at an approved landfill site. Composting, if done correctly with sustained temperatures of over 55°C, will also kill many pests and pathogens, including *P. ramorum.*

Last, but no mean least, is the need to improve awareness via education at all levels. The essential need for better garden hygiene and pest and disease recognition and prevention has slipped. My personal view is that it is partly because of the vast increase in other tasks expected of the professional gardener these days such as health and safety, interpretation, budget management and so on. If we are to truly make a difference longer term we need to in-bed these practices back into our day-to-day garden management.

So, simple recommendations might be: that garden staff (gardeners, volunteers etc) should receive basic training in the main pests and diseases of plants relevant to their garden. The general condition and health of plants should be monitored regularly so that problems are spotted early and prompt remedial action can be taken. Report all suspicious symptoms to Fera or The Forestry Commission (it is a legal requirement to notify all suspect findings of quarantine pests and pathogens to Fera).

HORIZON SCANNING

The risk from new harmful organisms is increasing at an exponential rate due to a variety of reasons such as increases in global trade (including plants), also the ease with which we ourselves can travel around the world. There are more exotic sources and more exotic plants/food than ever before. We are routinely importing larger plants and increasing the demand for cheap plants and food. A stretched plant health system built on visual inspection and known risks (ie already on a interception list) can only exacerbate the situation.

The pathways for these harmful organisms are obvious: allowing them to move from country to country puts at risk trees and plants within the historic, natural and urban environments, together with commercial trade or food production.

So, although this article covers *P. ramorum*, the lessons and techniques we have learnt can be applied to other threats, both known and unknown.

Although not currently a notifiable organism (covered by legislation) there have been significant losses of horse chestnut (*Aesculus hippocastanum*) trees from Chestnut Bleeding Canker. Similarly, we need to establish a clearer picture of how Acute Oak Decline is affecting our most iconic tree species, the English Oak (*Quercus robur*).

Box blight continues to affect our native box (*Buxus sempervirens*) and garden plantings. Red Band Needle Blight is now affecting pines throughout much of the UK and Fuchsia Gall Mite has been found in gardens throughout the south and southwest during 2011.

New pests and diseases that also pose a great risk to our green assets are: Ash Dieback (*Chalara fraxinea*) is the most recent and perhaps the most deadly arrival, posing a very serious risk to another of our great natives, *Fraxinus excelsior*; Citrus and Asian Longhorn Beetles (ALB) – in 2012 there was an outbreak of ALB, one of the world's most devastating tree pests, in the southeast of England, thought to have arrived on imported wooden packaging material from the Far

RHODODENDRON 'JOHNNIE JOHNSTON' is another microprop success that has safeguarded this rare and beautiful double pink maddenia hybrid

NATIONAL TRUST

East; Emerald Ash Borer, already around the Moscow area; and *Phytophthora lateralis, Phytopthora austrocedrae,* Chestnut Blight and Oak Processionary Moth are all part of this cheery new bunch here already or heading our way.

So what if anything can we do? I say: challenge ourselves to what we might do in our own small way to reduce this risk. A key part of the Government's new Tree Health & Plant Biosecurity Action Plan focuses on behaviour change and increasing public awareness, alongside increasing research, practical actions and improving import controls. I ask how many people reading this article understand what plant material they are permitted to bring back with them from trips abroad or take overseas with them, but conversely, I am sure many will have heard about the strict biosecurity procedures imposed if visiting New Zealand. For us it's a less than clear picture as we have a large boundary in terms of plant health, being part of the EU. This in itself would not solve all the problems we face but does form part of a complex jigsaw, which includes supporting our own growers and thinking about the

need to protect and enhance the diverse nature of our ornamental and natural plant communities. Personally, I would prefer to lead by example and play my own part rather than just expect others to do the work for me in protecting the plants and places that are so special to me.

MORE INFORMATION AND HOW YOU CAN HELP

National Trust
http://www.nationaltrust.org.uk/what-we-do/what-we-protect/gardens-and-parks/

FERA
http://www.fera.defra.gov.uk/plants/plantHealth/pestsDiseases/phytophthora/pRamorum/

The Forestry Commission
http://www.forestry.gov.uk/pramorum

FERA. Best Practice Protocols
http://www.fera.defra.gov.uk/plants/plantHealth/treeHealth.cfm

Plant Network
http://plantnetwork.org/category/links/plant-health-links/

Duchy College
http://www.cornwall.ac.uk/duchy/index.php?page=_News&subpage=_Latest_News&pagetype=item&refer=home&newsid=3026

Ian Wright
is Garden Consultant & Plant Health Adviser for the National Trust

Ros Smith
is Micropropagation Manager, Rare Plants Project, Duchy College, Rosewarne

Ann Payne
is Higher Plant Health Officer, FERA

Chris Trimmer
is Nursery Manager, National Trust Plant Conservation Centre

Franklyn Tancock
is Plant Collections Curator, the National Trust

Current taxonomy: *Rhododendron seranicum* J.J.SM. ssp. *sparsihirtus* ARGENT subspecies nova

GEORGE ARGENT

RHODODENDRON SERANICUM SSP. SPARSIHIRTUS
GEORGE ARGENT

RHODODENDRON SERANICUM was described from the island of Seram in Maluku (Moluccas) in Indonesia by JJ Smith (1932) from a collection made by E Stresemann, a German ornithologist, towards the end of 1911. The type was collected from the Hatoemete Pass between 1500–1700m from 'primeval forest' on limestone, where it was described as abundant. Smith states 'The species is well characterised by the scattered leaves with a blunt base, large flowers with deeply cleft, glabrous corolla, glabrous stamens and a glabrous pistil.' He does not describe the colour of the type specimen (which was probably not recorded by the collector) but describes various colour forms: light violet from a Rutten collection from the Meseleinan Pass on Seram, 'flowers brownish-yellow, limb orange, salmon rose towards the border' and flowers 'fiery red' from two separate collections made by LJ Toxopeus from the neighbouring island of Buru (Boeroe). Sleumer (1960) extended the range of this species to Ambon (Mt Salahutu and Mt Tuna) and documented the first definite record from Sulawesi: a Curran collection made on the Palapo-Rantepao road, which was said to be slightly different, with a salmon-red flower 3.5cm long with distinctly biappendiculate anthers (Sleumer, 1960). Thus

R. seranicum has become one of the few Vireya rhododendrons which occur on more than one major island.

An Operation Raleigh expedition of 1989 collected living material of this species in the Manusela National Park, Maluku which is still in cultivation. This has bright orange flowers with a yellow star in the centre. The Royal Botanic Garden Edinburgh/Bogor Botanic Garden expedition to Sulawesi (2000) collected several specimens which accord well with Smith's original description although the flower colour was uniformly orange, (probably the salmon pink of some authors), with a yellow centre and tube. In fact they go violet on pressing and drying which leaves some doubt about the range of colour in the wild in the fresh state. These collections from Sulawesi are all very like an extremely glabrous form of *R. javanicum* (Blume) Benn. and certainly this species appears to be very similar, if not closely related, to the very variable 'javanicum' complex (Argent, 2003).

David Binney, an amateur botanist from New Zealand visited Mt Sojol, in the year 2000. Mt Sojol is a major mountain (3025m) on the NW arm of Sulawesi; here David collected a plant that he recorded as *R. javanicum* (Binney, 2003) from the lower slopes at c.1000m. The RBGE was lucky enough to obtain material of this from him which flowered for the first time in 2008. This plant agrees well with the description of *R. seranicum* except for the hairs at the base of the filaments, on the disk and inside the corolla towards the base. It also agrees quite closely to *R. javanicum* ssp. *schadenbergii* (Warb.) Argent a Philippine sub-species that was recorded from Menado in the north of Sulawesi (Sleumer, 1960). However the plants from Sulawesi have much shorter anthers than is recorded for *R. javanicum* ssp. *schadenbergii* from the Philippines and it seems safer for the present to keep that subspecies restricted to the Philippines.

RHODODENDRON SERANICUM J.J.SM. SSP. SPARSIHIRTUS ARGENT SUBSPECIES NOVA

DIAGNOSIS

Differing from the type subspecies in having hairs at the base of the filaments, on the disk and at the base of the corolla inside.

HOLOTYPE

Binney RBGE Ac. 20001339. from Indonesia, Sulawesi, Mt Sojol. c.1000m. Cultivated specimen collected 2nd Mar. 2010. BO; isotype E.

DESCRIPTION

Shrub to 80cm, stems spotted with small brown scales when young, quickly glabrescent. Leaves spirally arranged. The blade smooth, broadly elliptic to elliptic, up to 14 × 6cm, the apex obtuse to acute, when obtuse, shortly and broadly apiculate, the margin entire, becoming narrowly revolute when dry towards the base; base rounded to broadly tapering. Scales small, lobed without prominent centres, laxly distributed abaxially, similar but quickly glabrescent adaxially. Mid-vein prominently raised both above and below for c.4/5 of its length, lateral veins 6–12 per side, wide-spreading, slender, minutely raised above and below when dry. Petiole 10–15 × c.5mm laxly scaly, not grooved above.

Flower buds, conical, with an acute apex, c.40 × 20mm, translucent green with smoothly appressed bracts. Flowers 8–9 per umbel, erect to spreading, bright orange with a yellow centre and tube, c.70 × 70mm, the tube 30mm long, funnel-shaped, with hairs near the base; the lobes 30 × 25mm. Stamens spreading all round the mouth of the flower; filaments densely hairy for the proximal 8mm, glabrous distally, anthers cream, 2–3mm long, some with a short basal apiculus. Disk hairy, Ovary and style completely glabrous

The Binney plant superficially looks identical to the other accessions of *R. seranicum* from Sulawesi, only on dissection of the flowers can the distinguishing hairs be seen. Variation in the hairiness of floral parts in the 'javanicum complex' has previously been noted (Argent 2003) and it would not be surprising if other similar variations were found. The fact that Gunung (Mt) Sojol is an isolated peak suggests this particular variant of *R. seranicum* might be expected to have a restricted geographical distribution hence subspecies would seem to be an appropriate designation to draw attention to this distinct form.

This new subspecies grows easily in our cool, but frost free, greenhouse in Edinburgh although being from a relatively low altitude it would probably grow faster and better with a little more heat. The umbel of flowers is well formed and of a really bright orange, with a clear yellow centre. So far, it has mostly flowered in our winter months which is a great asset. Like many of the lowland vireyas it is quite 'leggy' in a pot and would benefit from more space, planted in a bed when it would no doubt 'fill out' and become a better shape. It grows in our usual composted bark which has a pH of around 5.5.

ACKNOWLEDGMENTS

We are indebted to David Binney who donated this plant and I am always grateful to the garden staff, especially Tony Conlon who successfully grew the plant.

REFERENCES ■ Argent, G. Species patterns in Rhododendron section Vireya from sea level to the snow line in New Guinea, 160–170, in Argent, G. and McFarlane, M. *Rhododendrons in Horticulture and Science*, Royal Botanic Garden Edinburgh 1–312, (2003). Binney, D. Rhododendron collecting in Sulawesi, Indonesia, 111–114, in Argent, G. and McFarlane, M. *Rhododendrons in Horticulture and Science*, Royal Botanic Garden Edinburgh 1–312, (2003). Sleumer. Florae Malesianae Precursores XXIII, The genus *Rhododendron* in Malaysia, *Reinwardtia* 5: (2), 45–231, (1960). Smith, JJ. Ericaceae from the Eastern Archipelago XIII, *Repertorium specierum novarum regni vegetabili* 30: 162–178, (1932).

George Argent

is a Research Associate at the Royal Botanic Garden Edinburgh

Notes from the International Rhododendron Registrar 2012

ALAN LESLIE

THE SUPERB
FOLIAGE OF
RHODODENDRON
'CHERRIES AND
MERLOT'

FRANK FUJIOKA

EACH YEAR I END THESE NOTES with my thanks to the various national and regional registrars whose work in bringing together applications from their areas is such a boon to the operation of the International Rhododendron Register. However, on this occasion I feel I must start with this subject, since this season has seen the end of an era. Failing eyesight has meant that Jay Murray has had to retire from her role in fielding all applications from North America on behalf of the American Rhododendron Society. Mrs Murray first took over this task from another long-serving Registrar (Ed Parker) in 1985 and has served with distinction ever since, fielding no less than 3106 applications in the intervening years. I have become almost complacent in assuming that the data I receive from Jay Murray will be accurate and consistent, but these assumptions are almost always correct! The role is no mere sinecure and entails much correspondence with registrants, weeding out obviously unacceptable names and sorting out queries about descriptions and sending the polished versions on to me in a standardised format. This makes my part in the operation much quicker and easier, and in the event that I do have any queries, these have always been responded to with equal thoroughness and alacrity. I am keenly aware too that from time to time she has taken the 'show on the road' around rhododendron and azalea meetings to promote the registration process. During her tenure this process has moved from an exchange of paper between the two of us (we both started with boxes of index cards), to an almost entirely electronic mode of communication: only the registration certificates now have to go by traditional mail. Her contribution to providing and checking data before the publication of the 2004 Register and Checklist was also second to none, whilst her steadfast dedication to the integrity of registration data has been much appreciated.

I should also pay tribute here to her husband, Robert Murray, who I know has been her keenest supporter, for in effect this has been a tandem operation, with Bob's support skills on the IT side especially having been of special value. He has also been responsible for processing the large number of images received from registrants so that they are retained on file in a standardised format.

With customary efficiency, Jay Murray has been responsible for finding a successor to take over the reins: this will be Michael Martin Mills, who lives in Philadelphia, and I look forward to working with him. He is a retired newspaper editor, with many years of involvement in the North American rhododendron scene. His own two acre garden contains well over 200 cultivars. The RHS recognised Jay Murray's exemplary service in the award of the Loder Rhododendron Cup in 2005 and to mark her retirement the International Society for Horticultural Science (who run the entire system of International Cultivar Registration Authorities) has awarded her an ISHS Medal. In 1999 the ARS presented the Murrays jointly with their Gold Medal. I am sure that I do not have to remind members of the Rhododendron, Camellia and Magnolia Group that, just as was demonstrated so effectively in the recent Olympic Games in London, volunteers play an essential part in all our activities and need to be treasured!

Meanwhile, on the numbers front we received 171 new registrations in 2011, but the current year's figure is still a rather modest 64 (as of August 2012). The latter are made up of 39 elepidotes, 4 non-vireya lepidotes, 4 azaleas and 4 vireyas. Up until the time of writing there have been no special factors to bulk up numbers this year. However, recent contact with Maarten van der Giessen in Alabama, USA, has provided the very welcome news that he is considering the formal registration of all the extant, named, deciduous and evergreen azaleas bred since 1969 by the late Eugene Aromi, formerly a Professor of Education at the University of Southern Alabama. Mr van der Giessen worked with Aromi on this project and not only has many of the plants, but inherited the relevant breeding records. He is still evaluating some of the last seedlings and the van der Giessen Nursery is

intending to put some into commercial production. Collections of them are also being established in various arboreta, so it is more than valuable to feel that they can and will be properly recorded. Over 130 plants may be involved.

For the initial contact regarding the Aromi azaleas I am indebted to Herman van Ree, whose Hirsutum website (www.hirsutum.info) has already amassed over 7000 images of rhododendron cultivars. When new images are added to the website Mr van Ree checks the names against the published Register and Checklist and a note is made if the name is not registered. Through Mr van Ree's assistance I now have access to a collated list of some 150 unregistered names and will be gradually working through these, in the first place to get an entry on the Checklist for each one, but ultimately with the aim of getting a formal registration in every case. Getting an initial Checklist entry as soon as possible is important so that I can avoid accepting a new registration with a name that is already in use. There is clearly enough work here to keep us all busy for some time!

This might be the moment to emphasise the significance of the two elements that are the Register and the Checklist, as these have sometimes been misunderstood. Although the two are run together in the published work (and in the database) only those names which have a clear

THE EQUALLY STUNNING FLOWER OF
RHODODENDRON **'CHERRIES AND MERLOT'**   FRANK FUJIOKA

ABOVE & COMPOSITE IMAGE BELOW
RHODODENDRON 'NOCE BRETONNE'
JEAN SAINT JALM

indication to that effect are registered and thus make up the International Register. This is indicated in an entry by the abbreviation REG, followed by the name of the registrant and a year date. This will mean that the name has been checked for earlier use by the Registrar against all names then known on the database and that it was in accord with all the rules in the then current Cultivated Plant Code. Only those that have been through this formal procedure are registered. Other names found in use may be added as part of the Checklist and include anything named prior to the first list published by the RHS in 1958: the latter are indicated as INC: ICRA, 1958 (INC here meaning incorporated, ICRA being the International Cultivar Registration Authority). Although most Checklist entries will be an acceptable name for the cultivar concerned, others will not necessarily be unique or may in some other respect not be in accord with the Code, and their incorporation should not be seen as automatically giving them any approved status. However, where we know that they have been used, it is clearly desirable to record this so that the information is available and is there to help avoid any further reuse of names.

Many registrants now provide images of their plants and wherever possible the Registrar will have these printed out so that one may be cited as the formal nomenclatural standard for the name. This means that if there is any future doubt about the plant to which that particular name should be applied, then there is a definitive example to check against. It is a version of what the botanical world knows as nomenclatural types, although the latter must usually be pressed herbarium specimens. One hopes that one of the benefits of registration is that the information listed really will be definitive, coming as it does more often than not from the raiser or someone closely involved in the origination of that selection. What is shown in the image will usually be the fully opened truss, but occasionally, as in the accompanying illustration of *Rhododendron* 'Cherries and Merlot', it may be the foliage where this is an important feature of the new cultivar. In this case Frank Fujioka's new ('Pretty Baby' x *pachysanthum*) x 'Whid Bee' cross is named to connect the dark red flowers and the superb dark colour of leaf lower surface. Another approach, one which appeals at least to the botanical side of the Registrar, is exemplified by Jean Saint Jalm's composite image of his new

'Halopeanum' x 'Coronation Day' selection called 'Noce Bretonne'. Such an image is very valuable in enabling me to check that characters of flowers and foliage have been correctly recorded on the form. A second image demonstrates the appearance of the whole truss, and together with a third, showing the overall habit of the plant (not shown here), means that a really meaningful record of this plant has been captured for future reference.

New registrations in the current year have come from across the rhododendron growing world: from USA, Japan, New Zealand, Australia, France, Germany, Belgium, Norway and the United Kingdom, although it is slightly disappointing there have been no further new applications from China. As always there have been some interesting choices of epithets. Some which came from Alexis and Liliane Le Duigou might be a puzzle at first until one realises they are in the Breton language: 'Breizh-Izel' is the Breton for Basse Bretagne (French) or Lower Brittany (English), which is that part of Brittany in north-west France which lies west of Plörmel and where the Breton language was traditionally spoken and the culture associated with the language is most prolific. Another, called 'Penn-ar-Bed', is the Breton for one of the four departments of Brittany, which may be better known to some as Finistère (French) or Finisterre (English). It must be noted that using one of these translations in place of the registered epithet is not permitted by the Cultivated Plant Code and can only lead to confusion as it would all too readily be interpreted as representing another plant.

Relatives feature again in the choice of names, from daughters ('Rebecca Taffet') to grandchildren ('My Li'l Tonto') and wives ('Anne Marie de Beau Vallon'), with other references to pet dogs ('Maddie Mae') and a mythical Swedish princess ('Blanzeflor'). On a sadder note, several names commemorate individuals who died too young ('Joey Rabbit') or in tragic accidents ('Eric Szabo'). Gunnar Gilberg, in Norway, has chosen to name his new *R. auriculatum* seedling, 'Berkeley 89', to commemorate not only the locality (in California, USA) from where he collected the

RHODODENDRON 'BREIZH-IZEL'
ALEXIS & LILIANE LE DUIGOU

original seed, but the fact it was the very day they experienced quite a serious earthquake: he was very impressed that the next day, despite the general confusion, the rhododendron talk he was due to give went ahead as scheduled! I also enjoyed Frances Burns's choice of 'Noiret' for her new wine-coloured selection from 'Frances' x 'Purple Splendour'. Noiret happens to be the name of a hybrid red grape variety raised in the USA by researchers from Cornell University (and only released in 2006). The fact her uncle taught at the University for many years made for another happy coincidence. The old Waterer hybrid 'Purple Splendour' must be one of the most used parents in the breeding of new cultivars: the Register and Checklist has at least 300 cases where it is directly mentioned in parentages (and this does not count those cases where it is a parent of another cited cultivar).

Work will continue during 2013 to augment the coverage in the Register and Checklist of plants raised in North America and I would be very pleased to hear of any errors or omissions in respect of plants from this area. However, I hope I need hardly say that this does not mean that new information from any part of the rhododendron growing world will not be welcomed by the Registrar and that I am happy to try and answer any queries on the basis of the information now part of the database.

Exceptional Plants 2012

Shows

The moveable feasts that make up the RHS spring flower shows continue to impress despite changes in dates, days of the week, venue etc. 2012 was probably the last year that we will see both the Early and Main Camellia Competitions based in London for some time as the Society will not have the shows that host these competitions available, or at least in the form we have become used to. The Early Camellia Competition was once again hosted within the London Orchid Show and as I reported last year, this arrangement works well. However, for 2013 we will see this particular competition move towards the southwest of the country; this will provide an opportunity for gardeners in that most conducive part of the country to take a more active role in the camellia competitions and should have the added benefit of opening up the range of varieties seen on the show bench.

The need for increased diversity in the flowers shown is a particular concern of mine notwithstanding the fact that the general public visiting a show will always be impressed with the range and quality of the blooms. However, at recent shows the more 'expert' observer will have noted that the same varieties have dominated not only the prizes but also the entries for several years. Clearly, this is a function of the season and the plants that are actually available to the grower; let us hope that a change of location broadens the range of varieties on view.

This year's two shows each provided a good display; the early competition, as normal, was dominated by greenhouse produced flowers, but even so the number of staged blooms was relatively low. It is clear that if you have just a handful of blooms to enter and the effort of coming into central London is seemingly too onerous, the RHS shows department need to find ways of encouraging entry. The main competition was much better supported with a

PART OF THE 2012 MAIN CAMELLIA COMPETITION at Vincent Square   SALLY HAYWARD

strong entry in most classes despite the weather causing significant problems for those who chose to cut blooms early.

An interesting thing to note about camellia competitions for individual blooms is the quality of the staging, it is simple to think that all one is doing is placing a cut flower into a glass or cup, and of course that is exactly what you are doing, however, making sure the blooms are best presented in that glass is nearly as important as the quality of the flower itself; this is especially so in the multi-bloom classes such as the Leonardslee Bowl for 12 cut blooms. In this competition it is not only important that the quality of blooms is high and that they are well presented but also that the 12 flowers are arranged well with respect to each other. It could be argued that the winning set at this year's main competition were not the best 12 blooms but rather the 12 best presented blooms (*See page 144*).

VINCENT SQUARE

***Camellia x williamsii* 'Francis Hanger'** A medium sized pure white single dominated by a strong central, relatively tight bundle of golden stamens. This *C. saluenensis* Hybrid with *C. japonica* 'Alba Simplex' has stood the test of time as a resilient and reliable garden plant. Produced by and named for Mr Hanger, surely one of the architects of our modern approach to rhododendrons, it is interesting that it is a camellia that most successfully carries his name. As with all whites, the blooms do tend to become marked in the UK climate although its *C. x williamsii* self-grooming characteristics assist in keeping the plant looking tidy. For the white lovers out there try three plants together of 'Alba Simplex', 'Charlotte de Rothschild' and 'Francis Hanger', they will integrate wonderfully.

CAMELLIA X WILLIAMSII 'FRANCIS HANGER'
SALLY HAYWARD

***C. x williamsii* 'Mary Jobson'** A home grown, Caerhays Castle developed hybrid. To my mind this pink single has the best colour endurance of the 'bell' formed pink varieties of *C. x williamsii*, by which I mean that several of the pink singles fade rather poorly. 'Mary Jobson' is more resilient than 'St Ewe' or 'Mary Christian'/'Golden Spangles' etc.

***C. japonica* 'Cheerio'** Somewhat of a rarity or at least not commonly grown, this cultivar could be best described as midway between 'Lavinia Maggi' and 'Tricolor'. Although described as a medium-large in the Camellia Register the bloom shown was a small-medium semi-double with radiating red and white stripes and with a distinctive centre to the flower. If it could be obtained, I think this may be a plant worth trying for those who want stripes but find the two-dimensional (flat) flowers of 'Lavinia Maggi' off-putting.

CAMELLIA X WILLIAMSII 'MARY JOBSON
SALLY HAYWARD

***C. japonica* 'Mark Alan'** This plant is proving to be a stand-out show winner year after year; the deep red blooms fall outside the normal classification of a semi-double or peony form as in a good bloom the central petals are elongated and interwoven into what can only be described as something similar to red feathers, this effect not only makes the flowers appear very different in appearance but also

CAMELLIA JAPONICA 'CHEERIO'
SALLY HAYWARD

raises up the centre making the bloom much more three-dimensional. For the gardener, 'Mark Alan' is not just a show camellia but also a very good garden plant with exceptional foliage and good bud set; the buds themselves are also slightly unusual with flower colour showing through very early.

C. japonica '**Easter Morn**' A large shell pink semi-double, although its very high number of petals can cause it to have varying flower shapes particularly in cooler climates. For a large flowered camellia it does seem to be a reliable bloomer; it will not make a heavy bud set in our climate and it will probably be beneficial to remove some of those that it does produce in order to get the best blooms. However, it is still a good plant and a personal favourite. The flowers have a 'heavy-solid' texture that allows them to sit really well as a cut bloom for the home or show.

C. japonica '**Lemon Drop**' Good miniatures are always popular and it seems that those that do make it out into the nursery trade are, on an individual basis, comparatively better than the medium or large flowered varieties. I suppose the selection processes for a new variety are inevitably weighted against the miniature flower, so if it does get selected it must be extra special. 'Lemon Drop' is such a perfect miniature, with a formal double white bloom and a clear yellow or cream tone to the flower, which can become quite pronounced on an older bloom, although to be honest this does not actually improve it as it can make it appear dirty; however, the new blooms are exceptional. I find it to be a vigorous and easy to grow plant which benefits from regular feeding to keep the leaves dark green.

C. x williamsii '**Exaltation**' This is another of the mystery plants that everybody should be growing but very few do. Originating from Windsor's Savill Garden, this is a large flowered soft pink semi-double. The characteristic of note is that the petals are like folded or ruffled fabric, making them appear like newly opened buds for the duration of flowering. The central area of the flower can be disappointing as the stamens are not arranged together but rather form a random

CAMELLIA JAPONICA 'MARK ALAN'
SALLY HAYWARD

CAMELLIA JAPONICA 'EASTER MORN'
SALLY HAYWARD

CAMELLIA JAPONICA 'LEMON DROP
SALLY HAYWARD

grouping, however the best blooms have bright golden pollen which is a good contrast and lift the colour of the bloom. This variety has some worthwhile characteristics for the hybridiser to exploit; its large size and unusual petals in a formal double make it really interesting.

Although Exbury provided the majority of entries on the show bench for the Early Rhododendron Competition once again, there was some serious contention for places. Brian Wright stormed back into the event after several years' absence to take over a third of the 'firsts'. Not only was this a 'shot in the arm' for the competition itself, it also brought to the public's attention a much more diverse mix of rhododendrons than has recently become the norm.

Rhododendron **'Blue Diamond'** ('Intrifast' **x** *augustinii*) when seen in its true Embley Park form, rather than the inferior poseur often encountered in the trade, is a stunning variety. The compactness of one parent coupled with the colour intensity and shading of the other makes this a wonderful garden plant. The spray at Vincent Square really lived up to its name.

Another really reliable, yet uncommon rhododendron, which really ought to feature more in commerce is *R.* **'Phalarope'**, one of the Coxes estimable 'bird' hybrids. This one is the product of crossing the superb dwarf lepidote *R. pemakoense* with the taller Triflora member *R. davidsonianum*. The result is a lovely compact plant of soft lavender pink inheriting the flower-power of both its parents.

Once again Exbury managed to bring another of its exotic large-leaf crosses to Vincent Square, this time a magnificent hybrid, apparently of *R. falconeri* and *R. grande*, sporting very fine elongated foliage, a shapely truss and with a fabulous blotch in the corollas – yet another individual without a name that richly deserves one. Maybe micropropagation is the answer to getting these gems into more gardens?

CAMELLIA X *WILLIAMSII* 'EXALTATION'

SALLY HAYWARD

RHODODENDRON 'BLUE DIAMOND'

SALLY HAYWARD

RHODODENDRON 'PHALAROPE'

SALLY HAYWARD

Exbury have also got the knack of selecting tender rhododendrons which are star performers on the bench, timed perfectly, it seems, to coincide with the show calendar! Having assessed it now for consecutive shows, it is clear that **Rhododendron horlickianum** is another maddenia which other exhibitors should be adding to their greenhouse collections. Sweetly scented and subtly blushed, its blooms wide and generously borne – what more could woo a judge.

ROSEMOOR

The display at the Main Rhododendron Competition at Rosemoor in 2012 benefited enormously from the fact that the southwest had enjoyed a relatively mild winter. As a result there were truly magnificent sprays of tender rhododendrons on show, unblemished and in full flower. To see (and smell, in some cases) almost metre-wide displays of R. 'Lady Alice Fitzwilliam', 'Fragrantissimum', 'Bert's Own' and 'Dora Amateis' was quite remarkable and a great delight for the general public. The opportunity to focus on these tender rhododendrons may not arise again so forgive the indulgences here.

Foremost among the exhibits and of great interest was a rhododendron grown under the name **'Tyermanii'** at Glendurgan. The strong colouration of this striking variety is not mentioned in the description in the Register and it may be that this lovely cultivar's true name is lost or that a repeat cross was made with a particularly good form of R. formosum.

UNNAMED *RHODODENDRON* HYRBID (*FALCONERI* X *GRANDE*)   SALLY HAYWARD

RHODODENDRON 'TYERMANII' (Glendurgan form)   SALLY HAYWARD

RHODODENDRON HORLICKIANUM

SALLY HAYWARD

Two particular tender hybrids are of note, both of which were bred in Cornwall.

From Caerhays, it was especially delightful to see a perfect spray of **Rhododendron 'Saffron Queen'**, a cross between *R. xanthostephanum* and *R. burmanicum* which has excellent foliage and buds up very generously. It is hardy with me on Dartmoor but more bud tender than some of its type, so good displays are worth catching and the colour is refreshing and very pleasing indeed.

Possibly the most talked about rhododendron at the show was a maddenia hybrid which figured in the 2008 yearbook when it came under threat from *Phytophthora ramorum* in the garden of its origin – Trengwainton. Luckily its future now seems secure, thanks to micro-propagation (*see page 125*) but it was due to Marwood Hill's display and competition entries that **Rhododendron 'Johnnie Johnston'** entered the hearts of the public.

Double maddenias are few, but the pale pink rosebud blooms of this rhododendron are quite exceptional. Bred from the double form of *R. johnstoneanum* and *R. tephropeplum*, it is reasonably hardy once established, but easily propagated, so worth trying outside if an extra plant is kept under glass for insurance. Hopefully, this rhododendron will be more widely available soon to satisfy its many suitors!

RHODODENDRON 'SAFFRON QUEEN'   PAM HAYWARD

RHODODENDRON 'JOHNNIE JOHNSTON'   PAM HAYWARD

RHODODENDRON **'COUNTESS OF HADDINGTON'**
(Glendurgan form)   SALLY HAYWARD

R. CEPHALANTHUM SSP. CEPHALANTHUM
CREBREFLORUM GROUP   SALLY HAYWARD

It was most interesting to see the variability within the exhibits of *R.* **'Countess of Haddington'** on display. Whether this is due to climatic or cultural differences or there is in fact more than one clone in circulation is hard to determine. Whatever the reason, all forms of this *R. ciliatum* x *R. dalhousiae* are beautiful and its elegant foliage is an added incentive to grow it, both outside and under glass. Glendurgan's example was particularly fine.

An extra class reintroduced the opportunity to display a growing plant in an appropriate container. This had once been part of the Main Rhododendron Competition but overzealous entrants led to its removal when half barrels appeared on the benches with specimens many feet tall! Barry Starling and Russell Beeson led the way for what I hope will grow into a well-supported class in the future. Barry's demure and pristine *R. cephalanthum* **ssp.** *cephalanthum* **Crebreflorum Group** was an exemplary inaugural winner.

Shown for a few years now, *Magnolia laevifolia* **'Velvet and Cream'** has emphatically proved that there are superior forms of this wonderful garden worthy species worth seeking out.

MAGNOLIA LAEVIFOLIA **'VELVET AND CREAM'**
                                    SALLY HAYWARD

Contributions by Andy Simons and Pam Hayward

Tours

LAKE MAGGIORE

White formal double camellias are perhaps the most perfect bloom and we had a chance to compare quite a few different cultivars of *Camellia japonica*, especially at Villa Anelli where several are grown together, including the old variety 'Vergine Di Collebeato' and the even more venerable 'Fimbriata' with its fine saw-tooth edge to the petals. However, it was the true quality and substance of **Camellia japonica 'Nuccio's Gem'** that really jumped out on several occasions and made us say 'What's that one?', so it's the one for me.

On the shores of Lake Orta, the Countess Mirella Motta showed us her garden, which was full of camellias. She has a superb form of **Camellia saluenensis**, a strong upright grower and a good rich pinkish-red. There is a plant of similar colour at Trewithen, in Cornwall, but sadly, it is a weak grower and I would love to acquire and grow this particular clone.

In the same garden we saw a perfect young plant of the unusual camellia species, **Camellia yuhsienensis**. The single white flowers are quite loose and the hanging leaves with rusty-coloured undersides almost make it look like a michelia on first sight. Dr Kaoru Hagiya used it with *C.* x *hiemalis* 'Shishigashira' to produce his well-known hybrid 'Yume'.

CAMELLIA JAPONICA 'NUCCIO'S GEM' at Villa Anelli
CAMELLIA SALUENENSIS & *C. YUHSIENENSIS* at Villa Motta
EVERARD DANIEL

At the famous Villa Taranto, created by Captain Neil McEachern on the shores of Lake Maggiore, we were intrigued to see **Rhododendron leucaspis**, which one thinks of as a compact rockery-type plant, growing epiphytically out of a large hole three metres up in the trunk of a sweet chestnut tree (*Castanea sativa*). It had been planted there deliberately, and become rather straggly, but was very effective and unusual. It is sometimes epiphytic in its native SE Tibet.

Of course, we simply had to visit the Eisenhuts' wonderful collection of magnolias at their nursery in Switzerland and we saw so many of the remarkable new colours. Yet most votes went to the mature tree of my favourite – **Magnolia 'Darjeeling'** – so called as the parent tree grows in the Botanic Gardens there. It is one of the latest flowering and reddest of all the pure *M. campbellii* clones, though it fades to a purplish pink with age and, alas, the tepals do open right out and hang, losing the perfection of the opening bowl-shape. *M.* 'Betty Jessel' is a seedling from it, and I struggle to see any difference. Mine is at the top of my garden but, given the choice, make sure you plant either variety down at the bottom of your steeply sloping garden, so you look straight out into the crown of the tree, with the view across the lake behind, of course!

Contribution by Everard Daniel

RHODODENDRON LEUCASPIS (*and close-up*) at Villa Taranto
MAGNOLIA **'DARJEELING'** at Eisenhut Nursery

EVERARD DANIEL

Challenge Cup Winners 2012

ALAN HARDY CHALLENGE SALVER
Awarded at the Early Rhododendron Competition to the exhibitor attaining the most points.
Mr John Anderson, Exbury Gardens

Three of the winning exhibits that contributed to the award

R. 'OUR KATE MARISE'
SALLY HAYWARD

R. THOMSONII
SALLY HAYWARD

UNNAMED HYBRID (*PRAESTANS X MACBEANUM*)   SALLY HAYWARD

THE LIONEL de ROTHSCHILD CHALLENGE CUP
The best exhibit of one truss of each of six species shown in Class 1 of the Main Rhododendron Competition.
Mr John Anderson, Exbury Gardens

Rhododendron annae
R. arboreum
R. hookeri
R. morii
R. oreodoxa var. *fargesii*
R. parryae

THREE OF THE WINNING SPECIES *(LEFT TO RIGHT):*
R. HOOKERI, R. MORII & R. OREODOXA VAR. FARGESII

PAM HAYWARD

THE MCLAREN CHALLENGE CUP

The best exhibit of any species of rhododendron, one truss shown in Class 3 of the Main Rhododendron Competition.
Mr John Anderson, Exbury Gardens

Rhododendron semnoides
F25639

RHODODENDRON SEMNOIDES **F25639**   SALLY HAYWARD

THE ROZA STEVENSON CHALLENGE CUP

The best exhibit of any species of rhododendron, one spray or branch with one or more than one truss shown in Class 4 of the Main Rhododendron Competition.
Mr John Anderson, Exbury Gardens

Rhododendron quinquefolium
'Five Arrows'

RHODODENDRON QUINQUEFOLIUM **'FIVE ARROWS'**   PAM HAYWARD

THE LODER CHALLENGE CUP

The best exhibit of any hybrid rhododendron, one truss shown in Class 34 of the Main Rhododendron Competition.
Mrs Pat Bucknell

Rhododendron 'Phyllis Korn'

RHODODENDRON 'PHYLLIS KORN'   PAM HAYWARD

THE CROSFIELD CHALLENGE CUP

The best exhibit of three rhododendrons, raised by or in the garden of the exhibitor, one truss of each shown in Class 36 of the Main Rhododendron Competition.
Mr John Anderson, Exbury Gardens

R. 'Aurora'
R. 'Carita Golden Dream'
R. 'Gibraltar'

R. 'CARITA GOLDEN DREAM', *R.* 'AURORA' & *R.* 'GIBRALTAR'   SALLY HAYWARD

LEFT TO RIGHT:

TOP ROW:
'MARK ALAN'
'VALENTINE DAY'
'MRS D W DAVIS'

SECOND ROW:
'DEBBIE'
'NUCCIO'S GEM'
'ANTICIPATION'

THIRD ROW:
'WALTZ TIME'
'TRICOLOR'
'GAY TIME'

BOTTOM ROW:
'AARON'S RUBY'
'LEMON DROP'
'TAKANINI'

SALLY HAYWARD

The Leonardslee Bowl

THE LEONARDSLEE BOWL
The best exhibit of twelve cultivars of camellias, one bloom of each shown in Class 10 of the Main Camellia Competition
Mr Andrew Simons

Camellias:
'Aarons Ruby', 'Anticipation', 'Debbie', 'Gay Time', 'Lemon Drop', 'Mark Alan', 'Mrs D W Davis'. 'Nuccio's Gem', 'Takanini', 'Tricolor', 'Valentine Day', 'Waltz Time'

THE JK HULME CUP
The best exhibit in the Northwest
Branch Show
Mrs Jean Hannon

Rhododendron 'First Light'
R. 'Ne Plus Ultra'
R. 'Thai Gold'

TOP TO BOTTOM:
***RHODODENDRON* 'NE PLUS ULTRA',**
***R.* 'THAI GOLD',** *R.* **'FIRST LIGHT'**   DEN HANNON

BEST BLOOM IN SHOW
The best exhibit in the
Southeast Branch Show
Mr Philip Holmes, Nymans Garden

Rhododendron 'Taurus'

***RHODODENDRON* 'TAURUS'**   SALLY HAYWARD

Rhododendron, Camellia & Magnolia Group

OFFICERS

CHAIRMAN
MR ANDY SIMONS Wingfield House, 11 Brinsmade Road, Ampthill, Bedfordshire MK45 2PP
Tel: 01525 753398 Email: a.simons@ntlworld.com

VICE CHAIRMAN
MR PHILIP D EVANS West Netherton, Drewsteignton, Devon EX6 6RB
Tel/Fax: 01647 281285 (phone first) Email: philip.d.evans@talk21.com

HON. TREASURER
MR ALASTAIR T STEVENSON Appledore, Upton Bishop, Ross-on-Wye, Herefordshire HR9 7UL
Tel: 01989 780285 Fax: 01989 780591 Email: alastairstevenson@mpaconsulting.co.uk

HON. SECRETARY (Acting)
MR BARRY HASELTINE Goodwins, Snow Hill, Crawley Down, Sussex RH10 3EF
Tel: 01342 713132 Email: barry.haseltine@which.net

HON. MEMBERSHIP SECRETARY
MR RUPERT L C ELEY East Bergholt Place, East Bergholt, Suffolk CO7 6UP
Tel: 01206 299224 Fax: 01206 299229 Email: sales@placeforplants.co.uk

HON. YEARBOOK EDITOR & ARCHIVIST
PAM HAYWARD Woodtown, Sampford Spiney, Yelverton, Devon PL20 6LJ
Tel/Fax: 01822 852122 Email: pam@woodtown.net

HON. BULLETIN EDITOR
MR JOHN RAWLING The Spinney, Station Road, Woldingham, Surrey CR3 7DD
Tel: 01883 653341 Email: jr.eye@virgin.net

HON. TOURS ORGANISER
MRS JUDY HALLETT The Old Rectory, Thruxton, Herefordshire HR2 9AX
Tel: 01981 570401 Email: judy.hallett@googlemail.com

WEBMASTER
MR GRAHAM MILLS Tregoning Mill, St. Keverne, Helston, Cornwall TR12 6QE
Tel: 01326 280382 Fax: 0871 433 7066 Email: graham@tregoningmill.co.uk

COMMITTEE MEMBERS

MR ERIC ANNAL 36 Hillview Crescent, Edinburgh EH12 8QG
Tel: 0131 334 2574 Fax: 0131 334 6191 Email: eric.annal@btinternet.com

MR M FLANAGAN* Windsor Great Park, Windsor, Berkshire, SL4 2HT
Email: mark.flanagan@theroyallandscape.co.uk

MR M C FOSTER vmh* White House Farm, Ivy Hatch, Sevenoaks, Kent TN15 0NN
Email: rosifoster@aol.com

MR JOHN D HARSANT Newton House, Well Lane, Heswall, Wirral CH60 8NF
Tel: 0151 342 3664 Fax: 0151 348 4015 Email: john@harsant.uk.com (*Publicity Officer*)

MR STEPHEN LYUS 11 Meadway, Spital, Wirral CH62 2AR
Tel: 0151 200 0265 Email: emailslyus@yahoo.co.uk (*Advertising Officer*)

MR THOMAS METHUEN-CAMPBELL Penrice Castle, Oxwich, Swansea, West Glamorgan SA3 1LN
Tel: 01792 390008 Fax: 01792 391081 Email: trmmethuen@yahoo.co.uk

MR D G MILLAIS* Millais Nurseries, Crosswater Farm, Churt, Farnham, Surrey GU10 2JN
Email: sales@rhododendrons.co.uk

MR M PHAROAH* Lower Tithe Barn, Marwood Hill, Guineaford, Barnstaple, Devon EX31 4EB
Email: malcolmpharoah@btinternet.com

MR M O SLOCOCK VMH* Hillside Cottage, Brentmoor Road, West End, Woking, Surrey GU24 9ND

MRS CHERYL SAPCOTE 103 Quinton Lane, Quinton, Birmingham B32 2TT
Tel: 0121 423 3949 Email: cherylsapcote@btinternet.com

MR IVOR T STOKES Llyshendy, Llandeilo, Carmarthenshire SA19 6YA
Tel/Fax: 01558 823233 Email: ivor.t.stokes@btopenworld.com

MR C B TOMLIN* Starborough Nursery, Starborough Road, Marsh Green, Edenbridge, Kent TN8 5RB
Email: starborough@hotmail.co.uk

MR C H WILLIAMS* Burncoose Nurseries, Gwennap, Redruth, Cornwall TR16 6BJ
Email: diana@burncoose.co.uk

* CO-OPTED MEMBERS OF RHODODENDRON & CAMELLIA SUB-COMMITTEE FEBRUARY 2012

BRANCH CHAIRMEN

INTERNATIONAL
MRS MIRANDA GUNN Ramster, Chiddingfold, Surrey GU8 4SN
Tel: 01428 644422 Email: miranda@ramstergardens.com

NEW FOREST
MR JOHN G HILLIER VMH c/o Hillier Nurseries Ltd, Ampfield House, Ampfield, Romsey,
Hampshire SO51 9PA Email: john_hillier@hillier.co.uk

NORFOLK, PEAK & ULSTER BRANCHES
Vacancy

NORTH WALES/NORTHWEST
MR C E J BRABIN Rosewood, Puddington Village, Neston, Merseyside CH64 5SS
Tel: 0151 353 1193 Email: angela.brabin@btinternet.com

SOUTHEAST
MR BARRY HASELTINE Goodwins, Snow Hill, Crawley Down, Sussex RH10 3EF
Tel: 01342 713132 Email: barry.haseltine@which.net

SOUTHWEST
MR COLIN H T BROWN West Winds, Lustleigh, Newton Abbot, Devon TQ13 9TR
Tel: 01647 277268 Email: marylou@lustleigh.plus.com

WESSEX
MRS MIRANDA GUNN Ramster, Chiddingfold, Surrey GU8 4SN
Tel: 01428 644422 Fax: 01428 658345 Email: miranda@ramstergardens.com

WEST MIDLANDS
MR ALASTAIR T STEVENSON Appledore, Upton Bishop, Ross-on-Wye, Herefordshire HR9 7UL
Tel: 01989 780285 Fax: 01989 780591 Email: AlastairStevenson@mpaconsulting.co.uk

CONVENOR OF GROUP SEED BANK

MRS JULIE ATKINSON 184 Crow Lane East, Newton-le-Willows, St Helens, Merseyside WA12 9UA
Email: julie.soundgardenrhododendrons@hotmail.co.uk

WEBSITE: www.rhodogroup-rhs.org

Index

CAMELLIA JAPONICA 'PARKSII' A scented variety,
seen here at Chiswick house   SALLY HAYWARD

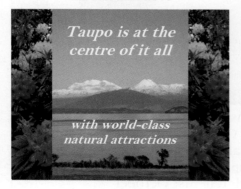

Free admission for RHS Members

RHS GARDEN **ROSEMOOR**

RHS NATIONAL EARLY CAMELLIA SHOW
16 and 17 March

RHS NATIONAL RHODODENDRON SHOW
20 and 21 April

Saturday 11.30am (after judging) to 4pm and Sunday 10am to 4pm
The competitions are free to enter although normal garden admission applies.
Competition entry forms are available from georginabarter@rhs.org.uk

Royal Horticultural Society

Sharing the best in Gardening

rhs.org.uk/rosemoor

01805 626800